Atelier Le Tallec™ Hand Painted Limoges Porcelain

Schiffer Publishing Ltd®
4880 Lower Valley Road, Atglen, PA 19310 USA

Keith and Thomas Waterbrook-Clyde

Dedication

To the many who have helped and encouraged us in the making of this book: Laurence, Claude, Beth and Ted, Sol, Jackie and Rob.

Library of Congress Cataloging-in-Publication Data

Waterbrook-Clyde, Keith.
Atelier Le Tallec : hand-painted Limoges porcelain / by Keith and Thomas Waterbrook-Clyde.
p. cm.
ISBN 0-7643-1708-3
1. Atelier Le Tallec--Catalogs. 2. Limoges porcelain--Collectors and collecting--Catalogs. 3. China painting--Collectors and collecting--France--Limoges--Catalogs. I. Waterbrook-Clyde. Thomas. II. Title.
NK4605.5.F83 A748 2003
638.2'0944'6624075-dc21
2002015777

Designed by "Sue"
Type set in Bernhard Modern BT/Korinna BT

ISBN: 0-7643-1708-3
Printed in China
1 2 3 4

Published by Schiffer Publishing Ltd.
4880 Lower Valley Road
Atglen, PA 19310
Phone: (610) 593-1777; Fax: (610) 593-2002
E-mail: Schifferbk@aol.com
Please visit our web site catalog at **www.schifferbooks.com**
We are always looking for people to write books on new and related subjects. If you have an idea for a book please contact us at the above address.

This book may be purchased from the publisher.
Include $3.95 for shipping.
Please try your bookstore first.
You may write for a free catalog.

In Europe, Schiffer books are distributed by
Bushwood Books
6 Marksbury Ave.
Kew Gardens
Surrey TW9 4JF England
Phone: 44 (0)20-8392-8585
Fax: 44 (0)20-8392-9876
E-mail: Bushwd@aol.com
Free postage in the UK. Europe: air mail at cost

Contents

Acknowledgments 4
Laurence de La Grange 6
Introduction to Atelier Le Tallec 7
Le Tallec Decorating Marks 10
Values 12
Le Tallec Patterns 13
Watercolors Painted by Camille Le Tallec and *Pots à Pharmacie* 15
Chinoiserie Patterns 27
Figural Patterns 46
Bird Patterns 60
Floral Patterns 80
Foliage Patterns 123
Geometric and Abstract Patterns 140
Animal, Sea Life, and Insect Patterns 157
Other Patterns 169
Auction of Camille Le Tallec's Personal Collection 203
Studio Photographs 226
Bibliography 238
Index 239

Acknowledgments

Most of the information in this book about Atelier Le Tallec—its history and its patterns—was provided by Laurence de La Grange, the managing director of the studio. She has been helpful, gracious, and patient; and she was a wonderful host during our visit to Paris to photograph Le Tallec pieces in the studio and to gather information for this book. We had the "run of the studio" for several days, and we were given access to everything we wanted or needed. We took pieces off the shelves in the showroom, in the museum, and in the basement and generally upset the gallery for several days with our equipment spread out and our unintentional rearrangement of many pieces in the studio. In addition, Ms. de La Grange answered countless e-mails from us over the last eighteen months. We would not have been able to write this book without her help.

Claude Souffron, who has been with the studio since 1962 and who manages the workshop, was also indispensable. She carries around forty years of the studio's history, and she was generous in sharing information about Camille Le Tallec, the studio, and the history and identification of many of the patterns. All of the painters and staff at the studio made us feel welcome during our visit.

We would also like to thank John Loring, design director at Tiffany & Co. since 1979, for meeting with us in New York to share information about his association with Camille Le Tallec and his role in developing several of the Le Tallec Tiffany patterns. Robert Headley, who oversees Atelier Le Tallec for Tiffany & Co., was also very supportive in all of our efforts to gather information for this book. He shared with us some of the history of Le Tallec, gave us leads where to find additional information, and told us about Tiffany & Co.'s association with the studio.

Beth and Ted Bodenschatz, who accompanied us on our trip to Paris, helped us immensely with photo-

graphing Le Tallec pieces in the studio. They helped us note the marks and dimensions of the pieces, helped us set up the pieces to photograph and gave us considerable moral support. They were great companions during the entire two weeks of our visit to Paris and Limoges.

Jackie Lowensteiner has been working with us for several years now. She provided us many photographs for our two earlier books on Limoges porcelain, and she has once again provided us photographs for this book. She has an impressive collection of both Limoges and Le Tallec porcelain, and she is always a source of encouragement.

A more recent contributor to our book writing efforts is Sol Labos Brien, whose influence is reflected throughout this book. She has the critical eye of an accomplished painter, and she is a perceptive artist. She has freely shared with us her insights into the art of Le Tallec patterns and the skills of the Le Tallec painters. She, in fact, has been our "guide" and "interpreter" during the most important period, the time when this book was finally taking shape. Many of our observations originated with her.

Sol has also provided us photographs for this book, shared with us her early personal history with Le Tallec porcelain, provided us with a copy of the auction catalogue of Camille Le Tallec's personal collections, and read and commented on the final drafts of this book. Her uncle, Ika Labos, and her father, Moses Haim Labos, owned an exclusive retail store, IKA, in Tangiers from 1950-1961. They only imported and sold high-end crystal, silver, and porcelain, which included Le Tallec. Because Tangiers at the time was a free trade zone and was a haven for many of the world's rich and famous, the family met many famous people at the time who purchased Le Tallec porcelain. One of the largest purchasers of Le Tallec was Barbara Hutton, the Woolworth heiress. The store, IKA, was later moved to Madrid and was in business there from 1963 to the late 1980s. Today, Sol Labos Brien is a collector of Le Tallec porcelain and is herself a porcelain painter who is influenced by many of the Le Tallec patterns.

Two other Le Tallec collectors, Denise Cote and Rob Glisson, have also provided us photographs from their personal collection.

We would like to thank the photographers, who in addition to ourselves, took the actual photographs for this book—Phil Degginger photographed pieces from Jackie Lowensteiner's collection and Jacques Francki photographed pieces from Sol Labos Brien's collection. Tiffany & Co. also provided us with several photographs.

Laurence de La Grange Managing Director, Atelier Le Tallec

Laurence de La Grange and her pet cat, Patapouf.

Laurence de La Grange is the managing director of Atelier Le Tallec. For the past twenty years she has been working in the "tabletop" industries in France. Initially she worked for a crystal manufacturer, Arts de Portieux, in the east of France and then spent some time with a crystal manufacturer in Munich, Germany.

Since joining Atelier Le Tallec as the managing director in 1994, she has overseen many changes at the studio. She managed the move of the studio from Rue de Reuilly to its present location on the upscale Viaduc des Arts at 93-95, avenue Daumesnil in Paris. She transformed the studio from what was a provincial workshop to a modern decorating studio, adding for the first time a retail boutique for the studio's own patterns and a view where the public can see the artists at work.

Ms. de La Grange has consistently strived to preserve the world renowned quality of the studio's work and the painstaking methods of hand painting porcelain, while at the same time moving the studio to adopt more contemporary designs and shapes, which interpret and amplify current trends in design and decoration. For example, in 1998 the studio decided to use models of little girls to decorate their Christmas tree. Three patterns—*Alice in Wonderland*, *Lulu,* and *Clowns*—were designed to complement the little girl motif; and all three patterns have subsequently become very successful.

In addition to managing the studio, Ms. de La Grange has made significant contributions to the creative development of new patterns. Her initial ideas usually come from books or from visits to museums and castles, where she finds a motif and adapts it to the shape of a plate or a jar. Each motif must further contain a story, like *Taj Mahal*, which is a story of a wedding in India. This pattern was developed when Ms. de La Grange learned that her daughter was engaged. The patterns, *Jardin* and *Siam*, were created after she visited the Musée Carnavalet in Paris, where for the first time the museum displayed the fans of Queen Marie Antoinette, which were painted by Jean Pillement. Ms. de La Grange was also the primary creative influence in the design of *Rue de la Paix*, a new pattern with icons celebrating the opening of the Tiffany & Co. store at 6, Rue de la Paix in December 2000. This is a chinoiserie pattern that is also based upon the paintings of Jean Pillement.

In 2001/2002 the studio moved to more romantic designs based on the French *toile de jouy*, and they experimented with landscapes and multicolored birds. On the technical side, they used more luster colors and different porcelain blanks.

Ms. de La Grange has been a major contributor to many of the new patterns developed by Atelier Le Tallec. She is inspired by the past, but she also provides inspiration for the future. Atelier Le Tallec will, no doubt, remain the foremost decorating studio in the world.

Introduction to Atelier Le Tallec

Although modern technology has achieved many improvements, it has not been able to match the charm, grace, and artistry created by the human hand. By refusing to submit to modern methods of porcelain decoration, Atelier Le Tallec has become the foremost studio in the world for exquisite hand painted porcelain, continuing a 350-year tradition in France that began during the reign of Louis XIV.

Like the royally commissioned French porcelain manufacturers, Le Tallec has throughout the years produced many custom made designs for the world's rich and famous. Although studio confidentiality prevents us from identifying many of these individuals, there are a few that are public knowledge. For the late King Hassan of Morocco, the studio decorated a formal dinner service of 120 pieces; for the Queen of Holland, the studio decorated a dinnerware set as a wedding gift; and for the Prince of Qatar, the studio has decorated several dinner sets and vases. When Camille Le Tallec died in 1991, the Prince of Qatar, a long-time customer of the studio, wanted a memorial of Mr. Le Tallec. He invited the director of the studio, who is now retired, to Qatar to paint a portrait of Mr. Le Tallec, and his faithful terrier, Buster, on the ceiling of his dining room. Although the director thought it was a splendid idea, she felt that she did not have the qualifications to execute such a task. Other known distinguished customers of the studio include the Présidence de la République Française, Danielle Steele, Marlo Thomas, and the City Hall of Paris.

The history of Atelier Le Tallec began in 1930 when the twenty-four-year-old Camille Le Tallec graduated from the prestigious Ecole du Louvre. Having completed four years of art history with a thesis on the Nast porcelain manufacturer and having grown up with his mother who painted porcelain, Mr. Tallec made a bold decision to begin a studio in the tradition of Manufacture de Sèvres. He located his first studio at 13 Villa Faucher in the unfashionable 20th Arrondissement, purchased a kiln and engaged a few painters to interpret eighteenth and nineteenth century decorations of birds, flower, garlands, and pastoral landscapes.

Around the same time he started his first studio, Mr. Tallec also began collecting eighteenth and nineteenth century porcelain as well as enamels. He purchased pieces that were not only an inspiration to him but also ones that could be used as teaching tools for his students. Mr. Le Tallec stated, "It was when I started getting acquainted with eighteenth century art that I became a modern ceramist." [translated from the French] When his collection was finally sold at auction in 1990, many of his pieces were purchased by French national museums, such as the Musée du Louvre.

Because of the urban renewal occurring in the 20th Arrondissement, it was necessary for Mr. Le Tallec to move his studio in 1978. For economic reasons, he considered for a time moving out of Paris to the suburbs. When Jacques Chirac, then mayor of Paris, heard about the now famous studio moving to the suburbs, he proposed that Mr. Le Tallec move his studio to a mansion at 67 rue de Reuilly in the 12th Arrondissement, the traditional neighborhood for artisans and the fine arts. The studio remained at this location until 1995 when it moved to its present location in the Viaduc des Arts.

In 1961 Mr. Le Tallec met John Loring, now the design director at Tiffany & Co. This was the beginning of a long friendship and fruitful collaboration, which resulted in the development of several Le Tallec Tiffany patterns, such as *Black Shoulder*, *Cirque Chinois*, *Escalier de Cristal*, *Directoire*, *Fleurs sur Fond Gris*, *Bigouden*, *Halcyon*, and *Coeurs Fleuris*. The circumstances leading to the collaboration between Tiffany & Co. and Le Tallec began when Bonwit Teller purchased Tiffany & Co. in 1955. The head of Bonwit Teller at the time was a man named Mr. Hoving; and it was through his wife, who had been dealing with Le Tallec for quite some time, that Le Tallec was introduced to Tiffany & Co. It seems only fitting that when Mr. Le Tallec died in 1991 that Tiffany & Co. purchased the studio as one of its subsidiaries but at the same time allowed the studio to retain its own identity.

As the head of the studio, Mr. Le Tallec was an authoritarian manager. Although he himself never applied a brush to porcelain, he scrutinized each piece, controlled the shipping of orders, and cleaned the kilns. All of his painting was done on paper, later to be applied to porcelain by his artisans. Mr. Le Tallec's temper was monumental if orders did not arrive on the promised date or if the painting on any of the pieces fell below his exacting standards. According to employees who worked for him, he was feared, respected, and admired.

Today, the studio continues in the spirit of Mr. Le Tallec. The studio currently has 372 patterns. Since 1993, however, when the U.S. banned pigments containing lead for dinnerware, a number of patterns either had to be modified or could no longer be made. Without lead many of the pigments are less saturated and not as brilliant. Dark reds and dark blues cannot be duplicated and the relief work which added dimension to several of the patterns can no longer be produced. Engraving with an agate stone is now substituted for the relief work. Patterns which are no longer made include *Halcyon* and *Princess Astrid*. According to John Loring, the studio tried substituting a shade of purple for the blue in the *Princess Astrid* pattern, but the overall effect was not acceptable. The *Marin* pattern is a good example of a pattern that is now made using an agate stone instead of the gold relief work. While still beautiful, it doesn't have the three dimensional effect of the original gold relief.

In 1993 Tiffany & Co. had to recall all of the pieces which they sold in that same year, because the dinnerware contained lead in the pigments. In 2000, Tiffany & Co. accounted for seventy percent of Le Tallec sales; in 2001, Tiffany & Co. estimates that they accounted for ninety percent of all sales.

Le Tallec has used the blanks from several different Limoges porcelain manufacturers. Castel Limoges made many of their rectangular boxes and blanks were also purchased from GDA. Chastagner for many years made the blanks for Le Tallec dinnerware until the company went bankrupt in July 2001. The Chastagner molds were purchased at auction later in the year by Tiffany & Co. so that the Le Tallec studio could continue to supply customers with the same dinnerware blanks. Tiffany & Co. and Atelier Le Tallec have now arranged with Royal Limoges to produce the blanks from these molds.

The Painters

The studio's painters still use the same techniques as in the days when Mr. Le Tallec headed the studio. All of the painters are women, and they are taught to paint with the hand raised high. There are still a few of the studio's painters who were originally Mr. Le Tallec's students, and they continue to support the traditions of the studio. A dinner plate still requires four hours of hand painting and an ornamental vase requires up to twenty-four hours. At least three firings are required for most pieces, and many hours are required to polish the gold work.

All of the painters at Le Tallec have studied in French ceramic schools. These include Lycee Auguste Renoir, Initiative, and the Mas Jambost in Limoges. The apprenticeship at the Le Tallec studio is two years, and it takes ten years to be an accomplished painter and to know all the patterns. The studio trains all the apprentices to have the "same hand" in order to avoid differences in interpretation when hand painting the patterns. The painter who is an expert in painting flowers will teach the apprentice how to paint flowers, the painter who is an expert in painting birds will teach the apprentice how to paint birds, etc. The painters do, however, exhibit creativity within certain bounds proscribed by the patterns. In a pattern with floral bouquets, for example, the painter will reproduce the pattern while at the same time show creativity when painting the floral bouquets within the overall pattern.

Until 1980 the painters at the studio were paid on a piecework basis. Although there were rigid quality control standards, there was the incentive on the part of the painters to paint as many pieces as possible. At times this resulted in pieces that were not up to the studios standards. We have, for example, found pieces in the *Marie Antoinette* pattern in the early 1950s where the painting was not precise and the blanks had blemishes. This, thankfully, is the exception rather than the rule.

Unfortunately, we are unable to publish the names of the painters whose initials appear as part of the Le Tallec decorating mark, since it is against the code of the Métiers d'Art to identify the individual painters of the studio. Atelier Le Tallec was inducted as a member of the Grands Ateliers de France (the fifty best studios in France) in 2000, and they are obliged to follow the rules of the society. The first rule of the society is to promote the *savoir faire* and art of the studio and the second rule is to prohibit painters from taking advantage of their positions as painters to promote themselves; rather they must serve the art of the studio. An atelier in France is a complete team of artists and technicians who all contribute to the art of the studio, which is viewed as a whole. The only important mark is that of the mark of the atelier, which signifies the artistic quality of the studio.

Savoir Faire

The quality of the overall decoration is made up of several equally important factors: the quality of painting itself and then the mixing of pigments, the testing of colors, and the firing.

Most designs require three firings—one for high density colors, another for low density colors, and one for the gold. Sometimes additional firings are required to rectify the coloring of a particular detail in the design. Each firing lasts seven hours and twenty minutes. The painting of the gold and platinum is very important in the decorating process. Both come out of the kiln with a dull finish and must be polished with brushes or sand.

The quality of the pigments is another important factor in the quality of the decoration. Le Tallec has its own recipes for pigments, and only three people know these recipes. The quality of the Limoges porcelain also contributes to the overall quality of the piece. The studio purchases only extra choice porcelain, with no defects like "orange skin," black dots, or irregular glaze.

If any piece decorated by the studio does not meet quality standards, it is broken. Unlike many other studios, there are no "seconds" at Le Tallec.

New Patterns

Each year in January the studio chooses a theme for the development of any new patterns during the coming year. In the year 2000, the theme was modern art and the studio searched for designs of flowers, insects, and birds. After conducting color tests, the studio paints a prototype, usually on a plate, which is best suited for setting up a pattern.

Launching a new design with different pigments is an arduous process. For unknown reasons, some new pigments will react unexpectedly and will chip off. After a month other pigments will begin to crackle, indicating that the firing was not correct. Multiple firings are required before a new design is launched.

New patterns for Tiffany & Co. often are created from artworks in the Tiffany studio and these are designated *Private Stock*™ patterns. New patterns may also be created at the request of a particular customer. If the pattern is not selected by the customer, the pattern may be included in the Le Tallec collection. On occasion the studio may simplify one of their older patterns for production or they make take one of the patterns drawn by Mr. Le Tallec that were never used.

Lately, the studio has created a simpler line of patterns. Because they can be painted in less time, the prices are somewhat lower, although they still must meet the rigid quality standards of the studio. In addition, the studio has been producing a larger assortment of small hand painted gift items, mostly for export.

Le Tallec is famous for both the design of its patterns and the selection of colors. *Rue de la Paix* is a recent example of both, combining both a chinoiserie motif with distinctive colors. The studio is continuing with the tradition started by Camille Le Tallec in 1930.

Le Tallec Decorating Marks

Nearly all Le Tallec pieces are marked with an *L* and a *T* in script. The Arabic or Greek letters above and between the *L* and the *T* indicate the year the piece was decorated. (See the accompanying production chart.) The letters under the *L* and *T* are the initials of the artist. When there are no letters to indicate the production date, the piece was most likely decorated during the period 1930-1940, prior to the starting of the dating system in 1941. From 1941 through the early 1990s, the production mark was changed every six months.

From 1941 through part of 1978, the Le Tallec studio was located at 13 Villa Faucheur. During 1978 the studio was relocated to 67 Rue de Reuilly, when the studio began using the production date letters beginning with *R* for Reuilly. In 1995, the studio again moved to its present location at 93-95 avenue Daumesnil and the studio then began using the production date letters beginning with *D* for Daumesnil.

On dinnerware pieces there are often additional numbers in either red or blue. The red numbers refer to the month and sometimes the day of production and a pattern reference. For example, in *07/770*, the *07* stands for July and *770* is the pattern reference number. Sometimes, however, the numbers to the left of the slash also indicate the day the piece was decorated. For example in *1116/223*, the *1116* stands for November 16 and the *223* is the pattern reference number. On other pieces with just blue numbers, the numbers are the pattern number.

Patterns which are made for Tiffany & Co. include the additional markings *Tiffany & Co. Private Stock*, and these patterns are exclusive to Tiffany & Co. In the early 1960s, when Tiffany & Co. first began selling Le Tallec pieces, some of the items did not have the Le Tallec decorating mark, although they were marked *Tiffany & Co. Private Stock*. For example, there are some bird plates painted by Georges Marchand that were ordered by Mr. Loring for Tiffany & Co., but they do not carry the Le Tallec decorating mark.

There are also several apothecary jars, *pots à pharmacie*, and a few other items in the studio that have a Sèvres-like mark. In starting out in 1930, Mr. Le Tallec wished to establish his studio *à la manière de Sèvres* and so used a Sèvres-like mark. He also wished to fool the experts, since he believed the quality of his paintings and patterns were as good as those done by Sèvres. This caused a problem with Sèvres, however, so these markings were abandoned.

Finally, in the captions to the photographs we use the format *AA/MLC*, for example, where *AA* is the production date and *MLC* is the painter's initials. When we were unable to identify a particular letter(s) in the production date or in the initials, we use a *?* mark.

Atelier Le Tallec decorating mark.

DATE PRODUCTION CHART

13 VILLA FAUCHEUR

A	B	C	D	E	F	G	H	I	J	K	L	M
1941	1941	1942	1942	1943	1943	1944	1944	1945	1945	1946	1946	1947

N	O	P	Q	R	S	T	U	V	W	X	Y	Z
1947	1948	1948	1949	1949	1950	1950	1951	1951	1952	1952	1953	1953

AA	BB	CC	DD	EE	FF	GG	HH	II	JJ	KK	LL	MM
1954	1954	1955	1955	1956	1956	1957	1957	1958	1958	1959	1959	1960

NN	OO	PP	QQ	RR	SS	TT	UU	VV	WW	XX	YY	ZZ
1960	1961	1961	1962	1962	1963	1963	1964	1964	1965	1965	1966	1966

α	β	γ	J	ε	τ	7	θ	L	χ	λ	M	√
1967	1967	1968	1968	1969	1969	1970	1970	1971	1971	1972	1972	1973

67 RUE DE REUILLY

[illegible]	π	[illegible]	S6	T	√	[illegible]	χ	+	ω	RA	RB	RC
1973	1974	1974	1975	1975	1976	1976	1977	1977	1978	1978	1979	1979

RD	RE	RF	RG	RH	RI	RJ	RK	RL	RM	RN	RO	RP
1980	1980	1981	1981	1982	1982	1983	1983	1984	1984	1985	1985	1986

RQ	RR	RS	RT	RU	RV	RW	RX	RY	RZ	RRA	RRB	RRC
1986	1987	1987	1988	1988	1989	1989	1990	1990	1991	1991	1992	1993

93–95 AVENUE DAUMESNIL

RRD	RRE	DA	DB	DC	DD	DE	DF	DG	DH	DI	DJ	DK
1994	1995	1995	1996	1997	1998	1999	2000	2001	2002	2003	2004	2005

DL	DM	DN	DO	DP	DQ	DR	DS	DT	DU	DV	DW	DX
2006	2007	2008	2009	2010	2011	2012	2013	2014	2015	2016	2017	2018

DY	DZ
2019	2020

Atelier Le Tallec production chart of marks and dates.

Values

The values included in this book are intended only as a guide for collectors. Since the retail prices for Le Tallec pieces are some of the highest in the world, there are relatively fewer pieces on the secondary market when compared to pieces from the Limoges and other European manufacturers and decorators. Nevertheless, Le Tallec decorated porcelain is available to those who know what to look for. Many of the Le Tallec patterns in the U.S. are Tiffany & Co. patterns and are almost always marked *Tiffany & Co. Private Stock*. It is only within the last few years that American collectors have identified and have been purchasing Le Tallec pieces on online auctions and at antique shows and malls, and prices have skyrocketed.

Several of the pieces in this book are "one of a kind" and are not available to the public. In these cases, we have not provided estimated values. Le Tallec pieces are often erroneously identified as Old Paris or Sèvres. Finally, many of these Le Tallec patterns can be ordered new through the studio directly or through Tiffany & Co. if they are Tiffany patterns, although patterns containing lead are no longer made. In addition, there are many Le Tallec patterns that were developed specifically for particular customers, and these pieces cannot be ordered from the studio and they are not generally available.

Le Tallec Patterns

Atelier Le Tallec has become world renowned for their creative interpretation of old patterns and development of new patterns, their *savoir faire*, and the talents of their painters. The studio has made many contributions to the painting of flowers, birds, foliage, chinoiserie, figures, and geometric designs. Often two or more different motifs are part of the same pattern, so it sometimes becomes difficult to categorize a pattern according to its subject matter.

We have also provided more than one photograph of the same pattern. Often elements of a pattern may be omitted or provide a somewhat different effect depending upon whether the blank is a box, a plate or another shape. The size of a particular piece may not be large enough to accommodate all the elements of a single pattern, whereas the patterns are nearly always complete on the "shoulder" of a dinner plate or on a vase. We were not always able, however, to find a dinner plate or a vase for each of the patterns. When the studio creates a new pattern, it is often conceived and tested on a dinner plate or vase.

We will provide background information on the fifty-two patterns, both old and new, identified by the studio as their most important patterns, although there are a few of these patterns that we were unable to photograph. The studio provided this background information. We are including photographs of watercolor patterns painted by Camille Le Tallec and the patterns on several original *pots à pharmacie* that were used to hold pigments. Some of these original patterns were later modified and adopted as commercial patterns. We have also provided as reference photographs from the auction catalogue of Mr. Le Tallec's personal porcelain collection, where it is possible to find pieces that served as the inspiration for many of the studio's patterns.

The pattern identifications, which accompany the photographs, are sometimes the actual pattern names and at other times just descriptions of the design and colors, which the studio uses to identify the pattern. The latter is true of the original *pots à pharmacie*, which for the most part have no pattern names. Some of the names of the patterns are in French and others are in English. English names are used when the pattern is more widely known by its English name. At other times, the descriptions or patterns include both English and French words as described by the studio, and we have elected to use the names just as they have provided them.

Patterns which are exclusive to Tiffany & Co. are noted "Tiffany pattern" in parenthesis; the other patterns are studio patterns, which are sold by the studio to other retailers. Tiffany pieces are nearly always marked *Tiffany & Co. Private Stock.* The studio has about 372 patterns, of which eighty-two are exclusive to Tiffany & Co. Tiffany & Co. supports four main patterns—*Jardin, Aubepine Gold, Black Shoulder,* and *Cirque Chinois*, with Black Shoulder being the most popular. Other Tiffany & Co. patterns can be special ordered, except for those which can no longer be produced because of the ban on lead pigments in dinnerware sets.

Beginning in about 1995, the studio began designing simplified patterns that are less time consuming to paint and therefore more affordable to the general public. The most well known of these pieces are the animal shaped boxes that are painted in solid gold.

The fifty-two most important Le Tallec patterns, as identified by the studio, are as follows:

Abeilles Or (Le Tallec)
Alice (Le Tallec)
Attributs de Musique (Le Tallec)
Automne Boisé (Le Tallec)
Bagatelle (Le Tallec)
Baron Jordan (Le Tallec)
Bayeux (Le Tallec)
Bigouden (Le Tallec)
Black Shoulder (Tiffany)
Bleu Céleste (Tiffany)
Carousel Chinois (Tiffany)
Charmille (Le Tallec)
Cirque Chinois (Tiffany)
Clairette (Le Tallec)
Clowns (Le Tallec)
Coeurs Fleuris (Tiffany)
Corail Chinois (Tiffany)
Coral with Médallion Flower (Tiffany)
Crépuscules des Dieux (Le Tallec)
Directoire (Tiffany)
Escalier de Cristal (Tiffany)
Famille Rose (Le Tallec)
Feathers (Tiffany)
Fleurs sur Fond Gris (Tiffany)
Fleurs sur Fond Noir (Tiffany)
Guirlande de Fleurs (Tiffany)
Halcyon (Tiffany)
Harvest (Le Tallec)
Jardin (Tiffany)
Jardin de Chine (Le Tallec)
Josephine (Le Tallec)
Lubéron (Le Tallec)
Lulu (Le Tallec)
Madame du Barry (Le Tallec)
Marie Antoinette (Le Tallec)
Nuits de Chine (Tiffany)
Oiseaux de Sèvres on Gold (Le Tallec)
Palmier d'Or (Tiffany)
Panache (Tiffany)
Pastorale (Tiffany)
Polka (Le Tallec)
Princess Astrid (Tiffany)
Ronde de Cygnes (Le Tallec)
Ronsard (Le Tallec)
Rue de la Paix (Tiffany)
Siam (Le Tallec)
Soleil (Le Tallec)
Taj Mahal (Le Tallec)
Tulipes on Gold (Le Tallec)
Tulipes Royales (Tiffany)
Valse Bleue (Tiffany)
William IV (Tiffany)

The photographs are divided into the following sections: the watercolors of Camille Le Tallec, the original *pots à pharmacie*, pieces and patterns painted by the Le Tallec studio, pages from the auction catalogue of Mr. Le Tallec's private collection, and several historical photographs. The pieces painted by the Le Tallec studio are organized by the major theme and choosing the category for a particular pattern is sometimes arbitrary. For example, many of the pieces categorized under *birds* are also *chinoiserie*, some *geometric* patterns are also *floral*, etc. We just used our own discretion.

Watercolors Painted by Camille Le Tallec and *Pots à Pharmacie*

Cover and selected paintings of Camille Le Tallec's personal watercolor pattern book: These watercolors were painted by Mr. Le Tallec on paper during the periods when the studio was located at Villa Faucheur (1930-1978) and Rue de Reuilly (1978-1995). The watercolor and original *pots à pharmacie* patterns were taken from eighteenth and nineteenth century pieces found in books, museum catalogues, and other museum documents.

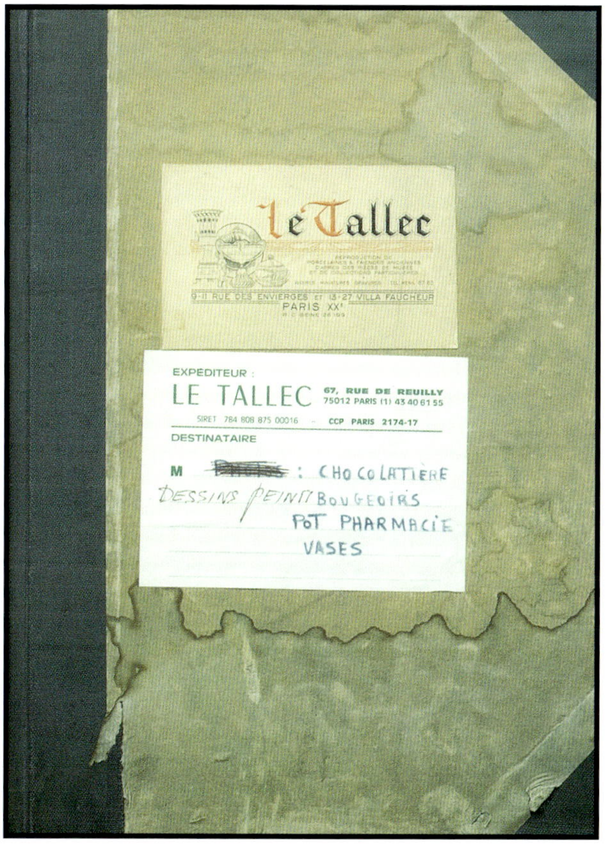

Paintings in margins were intended for the remaining sides of the jar.

CÆRVL
.CIX

VIOLA
LXXXIIII

ZEÆ
CoL.

Most of the patterns on these original apothecary jars, or as they are called in the studio: "*pots à pharmacie*, round or square" do not have names. When the studio takes an order to paint one of these jars, they just write a description of the pattern and the colors on the workshop's order sheet. These jars originally held different color pigments for the painters in the studio. In fact, many of these jars still contain the original powder pigments. The following apothecary jars, which are one of a kind, are marked with Mr. Le Tallec's "Sèvres" mark. The first letter in the descriptions is the letter within the "Sèvres" mark followed by the initials of the painter. Please refer to the previous original watercolors for many of the patterns on these *pots à pharmacie*.

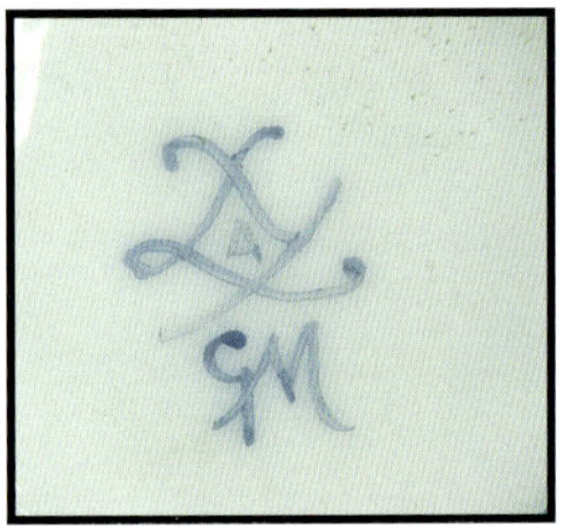

"Sèvres" mark on these original apothecary jars. According to the studio, the *A* mark may indicate the first year of the workshop in 1930.

Apothecary Jar, 11.5" high, A/GM.

Apothecary Jar, 11.5" high, A/GK.

Apothecary Jar, 11.5" high, A/AG.

Apothecary Jar, 11.5" high, A/GK.

Apothecary Jar, 8.5" high, A/CB.

Apothecary Jar, 8.5" high, A/AG.

Apothecary Jar, 8.5" high, A/GK.

Apothecary Jar, 12" high, G/GK.

Apothecary Jar, 12" high, B/GK

Apothecary Jar, 11.5" high, A/CB.

Apothecary Jar, 8.5" high, *Marie Antoinette Flowers on Céleste Blue*, A/AG.

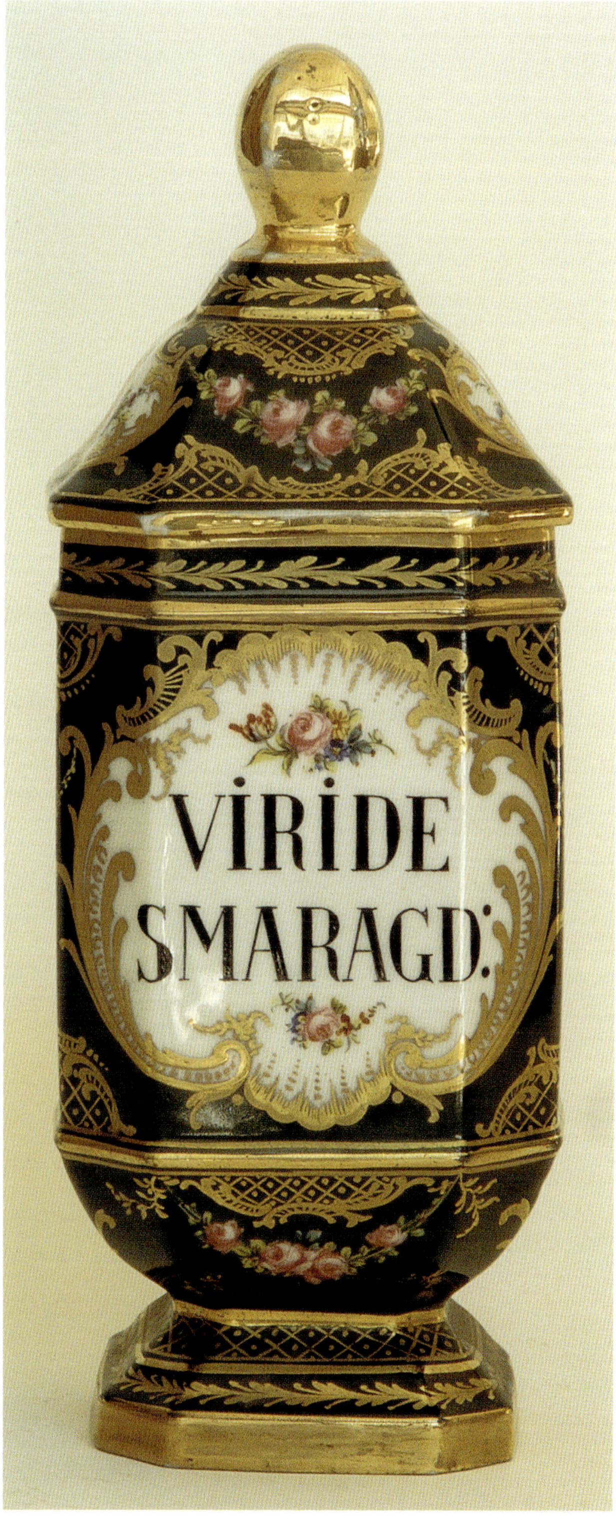

Apothecary Jar, 11.5" high, *Automne Boisé*, A/CM.

Apothecary Jar, 11.5" high, *Chinois on Rubis Background*, A/GK.

Apothecary Jar, 12.25" high, *Koi*, 12.25" high, G/GK.

Chinoiserie Patterns

Chinoiserie is derived from the French word, *chinois*, meaning Chinese. Chinoiserie is used to describe the European decorative arts, which were influenced by Chinese or pseudo Chinese motifs and which were popular from the second half of the seventeenth century to the early nineteenth century. Many of the Le Tallec chinoiserie motifs, some of which were originally based on interpretations of Pillement engravings, show a tasteful combination of gold and bright colors, such as in palm trees and dragons, that make them distinctive. (Jean Pillement [1728-1808], who traveled widely throughout Europe during his lifetime, was one of the most influential decorators of the eighteenth century. Using many different media, he is famous for his landscape, chinoiserie, arabesque, flower, and marine paintings.)

Candlestick, 6" high, *Chinese motif with Éventails* pattern, D?/CV.
$1,000-$1,500

Chinese Candlestick, 6.25" high, *Laque de Chine*, DD/VD.
$1,000-$1,500

Cup and Saucer, cup, 2.25" high x 2.25" in diameter and saucer, 4.5" in diameter, *Laque de Chine*, RB/JD. $500-$1,000

Candlestick, 5" high, *Poisson de Chine*, DA/CV. $500-$1,000

Jardin de Chine

This pattern was created in 1999 and represents the history of a theater in China with music players and actors. Pieces are decorated with either a vanilla or celadon background.

Ginger Jar, 9" high, *Jardin de Chine on Vanilla*, DC/CV. $3,000-$3,500

Box, 5.25" x 3.5", *Jardin de Chine*, DD/AG. Up to $500

Elephant Box, 6.75" high x 5.1" square, *Jardin de Chine*, DE/VD. $1,000-$1,500

Chocolate Pot, 11.5" high, *Chinoiseries on Gold*, LL/CLS. 1,000-$1,500

Box, 1.5" high x 2.6" in diameter, *Chinoiserie on Yellow Background*. Pattern was made at the request of the Musée des Arts Décoratifs. See photograph of mark. Up to $500

Cups and Saucers, cups, 2" high x 2.4" in diameter and saucers, 5.1" in diameter, *Chinese Landscape*, AA/GD. $500-$1,000 each

Cirque Chinois

Cirque Chinois was inspired by a late eighteenth century Paris porcelain piece in Mr. Le Tallec's private collection. Its polychrome chinoiserie motifs portray fanciful scenes in a rich palette of colors accented with traditional gold. The motifs are similar to Tiffany's black and gold *Nuits de Chine* pattern.

Teapot, *Cirque Chinois* (Tiffany pattern). $500-$1,000

Cake Plate, 12.5" in diameter, *Cirque Chinois* (Tiffany pattern), η/CC. Up to $500

Plate, *Cirque Chinois* (Tiffany pattern). Up to $500

Box, 5" x 3.5", *Cirque Chinois* (Tiffany pattern), RN/ALT. Up to $500

6.75" high.

6" high.

4.5" high.

4.75" high.

4.75" high. Dresser Bottles, *Chinoiserie Pourpre*, T/GK. $3,000-$3,500

Carousel Chinois

Carousel Chinois was inspired by a late eighteenth century chinoiserie piece of the Directoire period that was in Mr. Le Tallec's private collection. The original pattern was made at the Manufacture du Petit Carousel in Paris. Rich plum and gold colorings give the pattern an opulent feel, while the playful imagery adds a whimsical touch.

Five-Piece Place Setting, *Carousel Chinois* (Tiffany pattern), various production dates/ALT and CS. $2,000-$2,500

Plate, 6.5" in diameter, *Carousel Chinois* (Tiffany pattern), YY/AM. Up to $500

Consommé Cup and Saucer, cup, 7" handle to handle and saucer, 6.5" in diameter, *Carousel Chinois* (Tiffany pattern), YY/AM. $500-$1,000

Bowl, 3.1" high x 7.4" in diameter, *Carousel Chinois* (Tiffany pattern), WW/AM. Up to $500

Nuits de Chine

This classic chinoiserie pattern was originally made by Sèvres for the Semonville family and dates from around 1780, the end of the Louis XVI period. The design of *Nuits de Chine* utilizes the traditional gold of chinoiserie offset by a deep black background. The result is a regal design, which because of the black, works well in contemporary settings.

Box and Tray, box, 2" high x 4" in diameter and tray, 1.1" high x 6" x 4.5", *Nuits de Chine* (Tiffany pattern) RE/VM for box and RP/AO for tray. $500-$1,000

Apothecary Jar, 12.5" high, *Nuits de Chine on Corail*, σ (not a recorded mark, c. 1950s)/GM. $2,000-$2,500

Rue de la Paix

This pattern was designed by Laurence de La Grange for the opening of the new Tiffany & Co. flagship store on 6 Rue de la Paix in Paris in December 1999. The painters use an old hand painting technique to achieve a very deep red brown, which is similar to the color of an old print. The design uses "Tiffany yellow" for the background and sepia for the chinoiserie. Pieces in this pattern are used mostly for vases, which are on display in Tiffany & Co. flagship stores.

Ashtray, *Rue de la Paix* (Tiffany pattern). Up to $500

Cachepot, *Rue de la Paix* (Tiffany pattern). $500-$1,000

Box, *Rue de la Paix* (Tiffany pattern). Up to $500

Halcyon

The Halcyon pattern, created by Tiffany & Co. design director, John Loring, and introduced in 1980, was inspired by a small nineteenth century porcelain box decorated in a Japanese *Imari* pattern. The flower motif was reworked in pastel colors and the "Tiffany blue" ribbon was added, which modernized an otherwise classical *Imari* pattern. The development of this pattern started when Mr. Loring was visiting the woman who owned the English Halcyon Days company. She was showing him a large collection of her boxes, and he was particularly drawn to one of them. He took a small part of the pattern back to his hotel room and began experimenting with it. He then worked with Mr. Le Tallec to develop the final *Halcyon* pattern. This pattern can no longer be made because the blue pigment contains lead.

Box, 2.1" high x 3.5" wide, *Fontainebleau in Halcyon* (Tiffany pattern), RP/VM. Up to $500

Box, 5" x 3.5", *Halcyon* (Tiffany pattern), RC/SHF. $500-$1,000

Corail Chinois

The grand patterns of *Corail Chinois* are the same as those in *Nuits de Chine*, except here the classic chinoiserie figures are in gold set against a lacquered red rather than a black background. The original pattern was made at Sèvres for the Semonville family and dates from around 1780, the end of the Louis XVI period.

Egg Box, 3.5" x 2.5", *Corail de Chine* (Tiffany pattern), ε/OO. Up to $500

Siam

This pattern is an interpretation of one of the chinoiserie designs of Jean Pillement, who at the time worked exclusively for the King at Versailles. Chinoiserie was very fashionable in the eighteenth century as France began having contact with China, and the French used Chinese silks for clothing and decoration. *Siam in Green* became a Tiffany & Co. pattern in 2002.

Tea Set, teapot, 5.5" high; creamer, 4" high; and sugar, 3.75" high, *Siam*, DA/VD. $1,000-$1,500

Cup, 2.25" high, *Pagode, Or and Platine*, no marks. Up to $500

Flower Vase with Candlestick, 5.5" high x 4" square, *Kimono* (Tiffany pattern), DE/CS. $500-$1,000

Taj Mahal

This pattern was created in 1999 and was based upon a painting given to Ms. de La Grange from a friend who returned from a visit to India. The pattern represents an Indian wedding with a bride and groom, a peacock as a symbol of prosperity, and an elephant as a symbol of riches.

Plate, 10" in diameter, *Taj Mahal (Râjastman)*, DD/CS. $500-$1,000

Box, 3.25" x 3.25", *Taj Mahal*, DE/YM. $500-$1,000

Cachepot, 6.75" high x 6.25" square, *Taj Mahal*, DF/YM. $1500-$2,000

Vase, 9.75" high, *Imari* (Tiffany pattern), υ/ GM. $1,000-$1,500

Powder Box with a Fu Dog Finial, 6.25" high x 4.6" in diameter, *Imari* (Tiffany pattern), RG/G. $500-$1,000

Jam Pot, bowl, 5" high x 4.5" in diameter and plate, 7" in diameter, *Imari* (Tiffany pattern), X/GM for bowl and W/GM for plate. $500-$1,000

Box, 5.25" x 3.5", *Imari* (Tiffany pattern), ?/AC. Up to $500fa

Plate, 8.25" in diameter, *Fleurs Japonaises*, DC/MFN, special order for Monsieur Fraise. See photograph of mark. Up to $500

Famille Rose

Inspired by Chinese porcelain designs, this pattern was created in 1975 for Puiforcat, a silver maker and a famous store in Paris.

Egg Box, 3.5", *Fleurs Japonaises, Famille Rose*, ?/MC. Up to $500

Perfume Bottle, 5.75" high, *Japon*, marked *for Afico*. Up to $500

Figural Patterns

The Le Tallec figural patterns are exquisite. Figural patterns are very difficult to paint because the proportions, the facial expressions, the folds on the garments, and the shading must be perfect. Furthermore, it is difficult to paint figures accurately on small surfaces and surfaces that are rounded.

Plate, 10" in diameter, *Chinese Music Player*, marked only *Tiffany & Co. Private Stock*. Up to $500

Vase, 11.5" high, no marks, a sample made only for the studio.

Plate, 10" in diameter, *Chinese Music Player*, ξ/GM. Up to $500

Plates, 10.4" in diameter, *Chinese Music Player*, ?/GM, pattern originally designed about thirty years ago. See photograph of mark. Up to $500 each

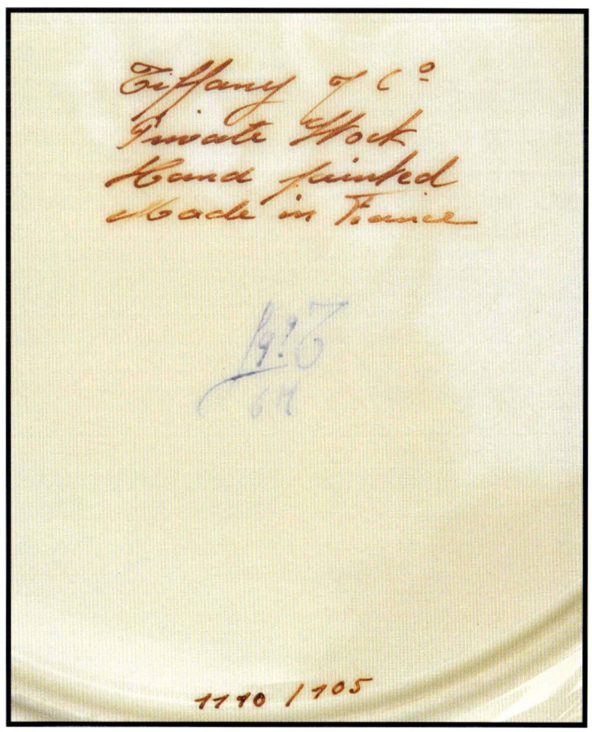

Jean Toth was a well known painter and architect in Parris, and he worked in pencil and watercolors. He is famous for his watercolor paintings of ballet dancers whom he portrayed both solo and in groups. He had an ability to give the dancers lightness, movement, and speed; and it is clear from his designs that he was knowledgeable about ballet techniques. Mr. Le Tallec helped several French artists and designers, like Mr. Toth, after WW II. The Le Tallec studio has a series of designs of dancers from the Opera de Paris, which were also designed by Mr. Toth. He was born in Budapest in 1899 and he died in Paris in 1972.

Plate, 12" in diameter, *Danses Africaines*, S/GM, designed by Jean Toth for Marin, a famous boutique in Paris located in the 16th Arrondissement. Marin closed about ten years ago. $500-$1,000

Plates, 9.5" in diameter, *Danses Africaines*, designed by Jean Toth.
Samples painted for the studio, υ (1976)/GD. Up to $500 each

Plate, 6" in diameter, *Spanish Dancers*, one of a series of plates with the same theme, R/GM, designed by Jean Toth in 1949. See photograph of mark. Up to $500 each

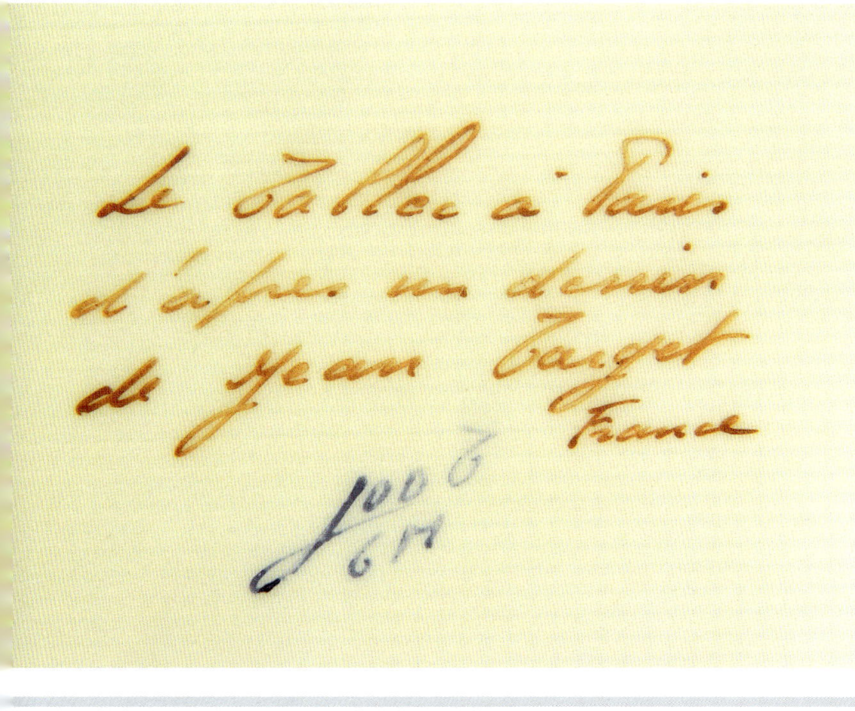

Plates, 10.5" in diameter, *Ballet*, *DD*/GM, designed by Jean Target, who painted many ballet pieces. Mr. Target's ballet pieces were very successful in France. When Mr. Le Tallec died, his daughter gave a full set of these plates to the Opéra Bastille. See photograph of mark. Up to $500 each

Plates, 10.5" in diameter, *Ladies*, designed by Touchagues, an outside designer. The studio has no background information about this designer. See photograph of mark. Up to $500 each

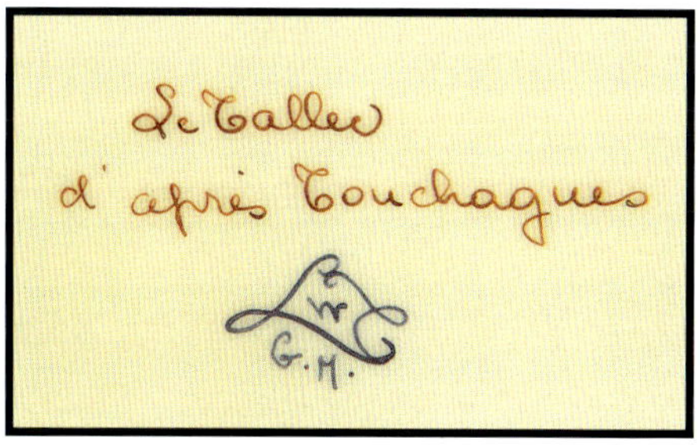
Le Tallec
d'après Touchagues
G.M.

Plate, 10" in diameter, *Jongleur*, RB/GM. Up to $500

Plate, 10" in diameter, *Accrobate*, RB/GM. Up to $500

Coffee Set, pot, 8.5" high and 9.5" handle to spout; creamer, 6.75" high; and sugar, 5" high, *Métiers de Paris*, HH/AG. $2,000-$2,500

Cup and Saucer, cup, 2.25" high and 2.25" in diameter, *Petits Métiers de Paris*, JJ/AG. Up to $500

Platter, 15.9" x 10.5", *Métiers de Paris*, an interpretation of a Porcelaine de Paris pattern developed by Le Tallec prior to1940, marked *Le Tallec Paris*. $1,500-$2,000

Coffee Pot and Sugar, pot, 9" high and sugar, 3.9" high x 3.5" in diameter, *Métiers de Paris*, Z/AG. $1,000-$1,500

Trembleuse, 6.5" high x 5.5" handle to handle, *Petits Métiers de Paris*, AA/AG. $1,000-$1,500

Cups and Saucers, cup, 2" high x 2.4" in diameter and saucer, 5.1" in diameter, *Parisian View in 1850*, JJ/AG. $500-$1,000 each

Plate, 8" in diameter, *Bourgogne* [Burgundy, a region of France]. See photograph of mark. $500-$1,000

Cup and Saucer, cup, 2.5" high and saucer, 5.25" in diameter, no pattern name, NN/GM. See photograph of mark with name of customer. $500-$1,000

Vase, 14" high, *Guerre et Paix*, depicting Napoleon's battle, τ [1974]/GM, signed *Grisard*. $2,000-$2,500

Vase, 14" high, *Guerre et Paix*, depicting Napoleon's battle, T/GM, signed *Grisard*. $2,000-$2,500

Cup and Saucer, cup, 3" high x 3.5" in diameter and saucer, 5.5" in diameter, *Abeilles and Guerre et Paix*, G?/AG, bees were a symbol for Napoleon. This piece was made only for the studio. $500-$1,000

Cup and Saucer, 4" high x 3" in diameter, *Battle of Napoleon*, II/AG and marked *Witepsk*. $500-$1,000

Cup and Saucer, cup, 4" high x 3" in diameter, *Battle of Napoleon*, II/AG and marked *Battle of Lutzen*. $500-$1,000

Bird Patterns

The Le Tallec birds are not only colorful, but they are complemented by gold and other background colors. Many of the birds are painted in a chinoiserie motif. The unusual color combinations are a unique Le Tallec contribution to many of these bird patterns.

Parrot Candlesticks, 9.5" high, RR/VM. $2,000-$2,500

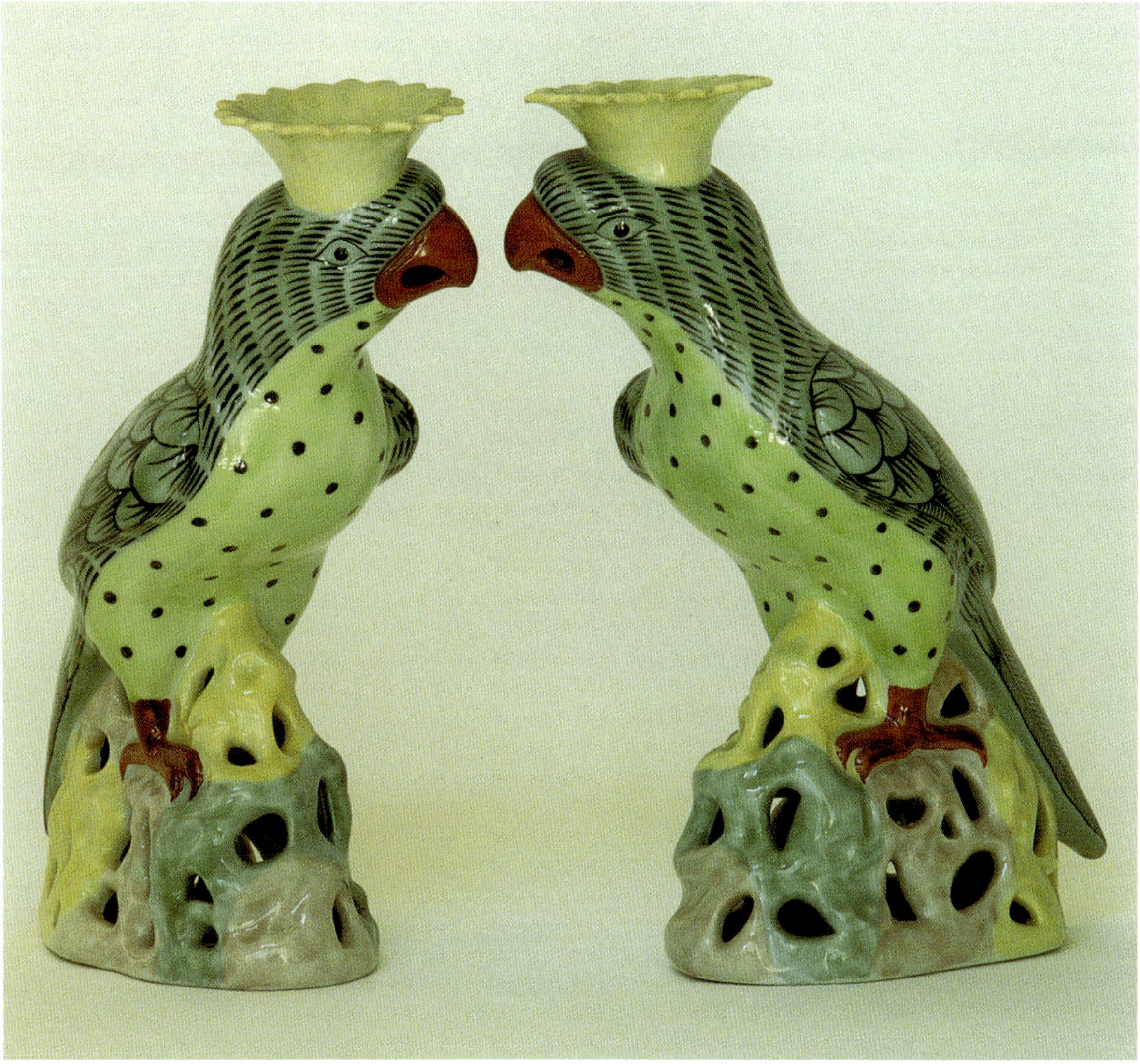

Parrot Candlesticks, 9.5" high, RR/G. $1,500-$2,000

Parrot Figurine, 8.5" high, Le Tallec mark in orange, a sample painted only for the studio by Georges Marchand.

Parrot Figurine, 15.5" high, no marks, a sample painted only for the studio by Georges Marchand.

Parrot Figurine, 14.25" high, no marks, a sample painted only for the studio by Georges Marchand.

Oiseaux de Sèvres on Gold

This design is based upon a traditional Sèvres pattern from the early nineteenth century, but the Le Tallec interpretation adds more flowers and changes the colors of the birds.

Bowl, 2.75" high x 9.5" in diameter, *Oiseaux Polychromes sur Or Mat*, GG/JL. There is also a brass ladle with a porcelain handle in the same pattern, 8" long. Both pieces came in a box marked *LA MARQUISE DE SÉVIGNÉ*, which was a famous candy in Paris on avenue Victor Hugo, which closed five years ago. $2,000-$2,500

Tray, 7" square, *Oiseaux de Sèvres on Gold*, DE/SD. $500-$1,000

Rolling Egg Box, 2.5" x 1.5", *Oiseaux Polychromes sur Or Mat*, marked *Le Tallec à Paris, France*. No date or painter's initials. $1,000-$1,500

Coffret Maurice Box, 4" x 2.75", *Oiseaux Polychromes sur Or Mat*, gravure à l'agate, K?/RG. $500-$1,000

Cup and Saucer, cup. 2.25" high and saucer, 4.6" in diameter, *Oiseaux de Sèvres*, JJ/AG on cup and GG/MCD on saucer. Up to $500

Ashtray, 6" in diameter, *Oiseaux de Sèvres*, α/AM. Up to $500

Jardinière, 11.5" handle to handle, *Oiseaux de Sèvres Polychrome on Red*, υ/GM. $3,500-$4,000

Scalloped Vegetable Dish, 8.75" square, *Oiseaux de Paradis*, τ [1971]/JN. $500-$1,000

Plates, 10.5" in diameter, *Oiseaux Européens à Manière de Buffon*, RB/GM. Up to $500 each

Plates, 7.1" in diameter, *Oiseaux Européens*, marked *Tiffany & Co. Private Stock*. The original design was created by Georges Marchand after the "Oiseaux de Buffon" and an eighteenth century plate bought by Camille Le Tallec. The studio believes that these plates were painted approximately thirty years ago for an order placed by John Loring, design director of Tiffany & Co. The original plates are in the studio's museum. When Tiffany & Co. first began its *Private Stock* designation for pieces decorated by Le Tallec, many of the pieces did not have a Le Tallec decorating mark. Up to $500 each

Vase, 3.5" high x 2.9" in diameter, *Oiseaux Européens*, dated E. Up to $500

Automne Boisé

The dark copper green background in the pattern recalls the first days of autumn, and partridges and pheasants fill the médaillons. This pattern represents the best engraved matt gold work done in the studio over the last ten years.

Jar, 12.75" high, *Automne Boisé*, DA/CS. $3,000-$3,500

Box, 3" high x 3.4" in diameter, *Automne Boisé*, DB/VM. Up to $500

Princess Astrid

This pattern's name comes from Princess Astrid of Sweden, bride of Leopold II, King of Belgium. The original pattern, which included médaillons of birds, was designed by Mr. Le Tallec for the wedding service of Leopold and Astrid. A band of pink and white hawthorn creates a striking burst of color against a background of the popular French blue color. The dark blue in this pattern, however, can no longer be reproduced because the blue glaze contained lead. The studio tried substituting purple and other colors, but the pattern did not work aesthetically with these colors. This was the first pattern designed by Atelier Le Tallec. It was later modified for Tiffany & Co. by omitting the polychrome birds, among other things.

(18) Serving Bowl and Plate, bowl, 8" high and 12" handle to handle and plate, 16.5" x 11", *Princess Astrid*, 1972/GM, original pattern. $5,000+

Plate, 10.5" in diameter, *Princess Astrid*, illegible date/CGM, original pattern. $1,000-$1,500

Pair of Urns, 18.5" high, *Princess Astrid*, μ/GM, original pattern. $5,000+

Vase Directoire, 12.75" high, *Princess Astrid*, φ/JN, original pattern. $3,000-$3,500

Plate, 9.5" in diameter, *Paradise Birds*, PP/GM. See photograph of mark. $500-$1,000

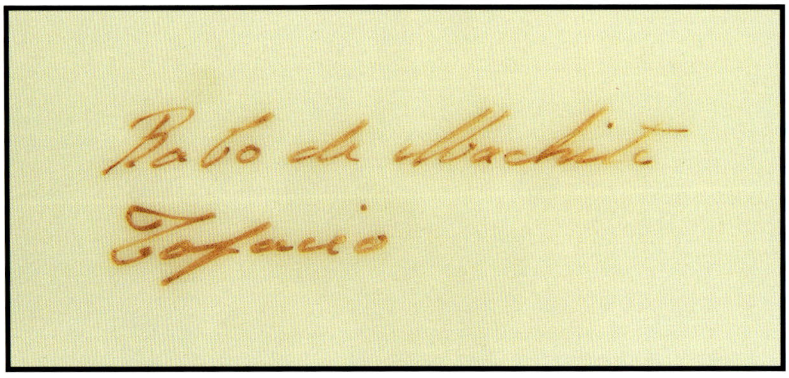

Cup and Saucer, cup, 2.25" high x 2.25" in diameter and saucer, 4.6" in diameter, *Modern Birds*, DD/CLS, a prototype. Up to $500

Box, 2" high x 4.25" x 3", no pattern name, ?/GM, marked *Tiffany & Co. Private Stock*. $500-$1,000

Box, 2" high x 2.1" in diameter, J/CC. Up to $500

Box, 3.5" x 2", *Perroquets*, RH/CS. Up to $500

Plate, 10.25" in diameter, *Paon*, AD/GM. $500-$1,000

Cup and Saucer, cup, 2.25" high and saucer, 4.5" in diameter, *Peacock*. DB/CS. Up to $500

Bayeux

This pattern is an interpretation of one of the most famous patterns from Manufacture de Bayeux in Normandy. Bayeux started in the early nineteenth century and was famous for its interpretations of Japanese designs. Bayeux was still using natural pigments in the nineteenth century, while the factories in Limoges were beginning to use chemical pigments. The original company was open for only a short time, c. 1810-1849, and pieces from this period command high prices. The company finally ceased business in 1953, and the last owner, Michel Morlent and his wife, Ginamy, gave a large collection of Bayeux pieces to a museum. All the flowers in the Le Tallec pattern are underlined with gold and are highlighted with bright colors—yellow, blue, and red.

Ginger Jar, 9.5" high, *Bayeux*. $2,500-$3,000

Cup and Saucer, cup, 2.25" high x 4" in diameter and saucer, 5.75" in diameter, *Bayeux*, ψ/AM. $500-$1,000

Box, 5.5" x 3.5", *Bayeux*, RB/CS and marked *Keith and Thomas Waterbrook-Clyde/5-11-2001* inside lid. $500-$1,000

Box, 3.5" x 1.5", *Pastorale* (Tiffany pattern), DD/CS. $500-$1,000

Pastorale

Created in 1998 for Tiffany & Co., the pattern was inspired from an Italian *trompe l'oeil* painting, which is located in a palace near Florence. The aviary is filled with polychrome birds flying among flowers and fruit.

Ronde de Cygnes

This pattern derives from an antique design created by Porcelaine de Paris in the early nineteenth century. The original piece was in Mr. Tallec's collection. The swan was a favorite design motif during the period of the First Empire, 1804-1814, and was also often used on cabinets, textiles, and furniture.

Empire Coffee Cup and Saucer, cup, 2.75" high and saucer, 4.5" in diameter, *Ronde de Cygnes*. Up to $500

Tray, 8.5" square, no pattern name, DC/CS, prototype rejected by Tiffany & Co.

Floral Patterns

Elements that make the Le Tallec floral patterns special are the combination of the floral bouquets, the choice of color backgrounds, the gold scrolls, and the colorful flowers. The patterns reflect a unique sense of color. While the floral bouquets on the same piece may at first glance look the same, they actually reflect differences on the part of the painters who are creative within each of the bouquets. No two bouquets are the same.

Plate, 10.75" in diameter, faïence, ZZ/CH. Up to $500

Plate, 9.25" in diameter, *Trois Médaillons de Fleurs sur Fond Rose à la Manière de Sèvres*, θ/SHF. Up to $500

Apothecary Jar, *Médaillons de Fleurs on Céleste Background*, 12" high, P?/GL. This piece was made for the studio only.

Perfume Bottle and Dresser Box, bottle, 6" high and box, 4" x 4", *Médaillons de Fleurs, Bandes Cobalt*, α/FN. $500-$1,000

Perfume Bottle, 5" high, *Médaillons de Fleurs*, LL/PP. Up to $500

Pin Trays, 5" x 3", *Médaillons de Fleurs*, AA/AKG. Up to $500 for both

Harvest

The inspiration for this pattern, which was created in 1999, is a hot summer day in June in the French countryside.

Tea Set, pot, 9.5" handle to spout and 5" high, *Harvest*, DE/YM. $1,000-$1,500

Madame du Barry

Madame du Barry was the mistress of King Louis XV. She helped to promote the Manufacture de Sèvres throughout Europe and was one of the most important Sèvres customers. The original Sèvres pattern, which this pattern is based upon, was created for Madame du Barry when she was banished from Versailles and went to live in Louveciennes near Paris.

Chocolate Cup and Saucer, cup, 4" high x 4.5" in diameter and saucer, 6.25" in diameter, *Madame du Barry*, DA/SM. $500-$1,000

Plate, 10" in diameter, *Ruban Rose*, DC/MYR. Up to $500

Covered Box, 7.1" x 5.75", *Ruban Rose*, DD/MFM. $500-$1,000

Tray, 7.5" square, *Ruban Rose*, DF/CM. $500-$1,000

Box, 1.5" high x 2" in diameter, *Ruban Rose*, dated RI. Up to $500

Plate, 10.1" in diameter, *Fond Plein Bleuets en Rose*, α/SHF. Up to $500

Ink Well, 5.5" high and 5" square, *Décor à la Rose*, no marks. Mr. Le Tallec sometimes gave pieces to apprentices for training, and these pieces are not marked.

Ink Bottle, 4" high x 4.25" in diameter, *Roseraie*, painted prior to 1940. Up to $500

Baron Jourdan

This is one of the most famous Le Tallec patterns. Baron Jourdan, a member of the board of Sèvres in the eighteenth century, requested one of the Sèvres designers to paint an exclusive pattern for himself and his family. This pattern, which is painted in a light blue, eighteenth century green or pale yellow background, is based upon the original Sèvres pattern. The flowers in the basket are Baron Jourdan's favorite flowers, and they all are different.

Tray, 7" square, *Baron Jourdan*, DF/MFM. $500-$1,000

Plate, 10.25" in diameter, *Baron Jourdan en Bleu*, RJ/MC. $500-$1,000

Ashtray, 4.9" x 3.25", *Baron Jourdan*, RRB/CM. Up to $500

Plate on three bronze feet and bronze rim, 6" in diameter, *Baron* Jordan, VV/NB. $500-$1,000

Marie Antoinette

The original pattern was created in Sèvres for Queen Marie Antoinette when she was wedded to King Louis XVI at Versailles. The pattern includes all the flowers cherished by the Queen. The background of this pattern was initially a ruby color accented with gold foliage, and the pattern was originally created for a large pair of vases and then later adapted to dinnerware.

Tray, 7" square, *Marie Antoinette*, DE/MFM. $500-$1,000

Bowl, 3" high x 10.5" in diameter, *Marie Antoinette Pourpre*, τ/MC. This piece combines two different patterns, *Marie Antoinette* and *Attributs de Musique*. $1,000-$1,500

Cup and Saucer, cup, 3" high x 3.5" in diameter and saucer, 5.5" in diameter, *Marie Antoinette on Rubis Background*, υ/MMF. $500-$1,000

Chocolate Pot and Tray, pot, 9.9" high and tray, 12" in diameter, *Marie Antoinette*, X/GD. $1,000-$1,500

Plate, 7" in diameter, *Marie Antoinette in Bleu*, EE/AK. Up to $500

Bagatelle

Napoleon ordered the original pattern from Sèvres, which was flowers on a gold background. The entire dinnerware set was given to King Maximilien-Joseph, King of Bavaria, in 1810. The original pieces are on display in Munich, Germany.

Tray, 7" square, *Bagatelle*, DE/MFM. $500-$1,000

Ashtray, 5" x 3.75", *Bagatelle*, η/MJ. Up to $500

Ashtray, 5" x 3.75", *Bagatelle*, η/CJ. Up to $500

Ashtray, 6" in diameter, *Bagatelle*, η/CJ. $500-$1,000

Pin Tray, 5" x 3.25", *Bagatelle*, WW/CCT. Up to $500

Powder Box, 3.25" high x 4" in diameter, *Bagatelle*, DB/SHF. Up to $500

Vase, 11.75" high, *Bagatelle*, DC/MFM. $2,000-$2,500

Plate, 10.25" in diameter, *Bagatelle*, ε/MC. $500-$1,000

Goblet, 5.75" high, *Bagatelle*, WW/PP. Up to $500

Chocolate Pot, 9" high, *Bagatelle*, DG/MMF. $1,000-$1,500

Tulipes on Gold

This pattern is an interpretation of a design created by Porcelaine de Paris. Mr. Le Tallec had several pieces of the original pattern in his private collection. Many pieces of this Le Tallec pattern have been sold to royalty in the Middle East.

Cup and Saucer, cup, 2.25" high and saucer, 4.5" high, *Tulipes on Gold*, RR/SHF. Up to $500

Powder Box, 3.25" high x 4" in diameter, *Tulipes on Gold*, DB/SHF. Up to $500

Demitasse Cup and Saucer, cup, 2.9" high x 2.25" in diameter and saucer, 4.5" in diameter, *Fleurs 18ème*, θ/SHF. Up to $500

Apothecary Jars, 13" high, *Fleurs 18 ème sur Fond Bleu de Sèvres*, X/GD. $2,500-$3,000

Plates, 10.1" in diameter, *Comte d'Artois*, samples made for the conservator of the Louvre, and marked for the Musée des Arts Décoratifs in Paris and *Tiffany & Co.* Note that the back of the rim of the plate is also decorated. See photograph of back of plate and mark. $1,000-$1,500

Plate, 10.1" in diameter, specially commissioned pattern, which is unnamed, ξ/FF. See photograph of mark.

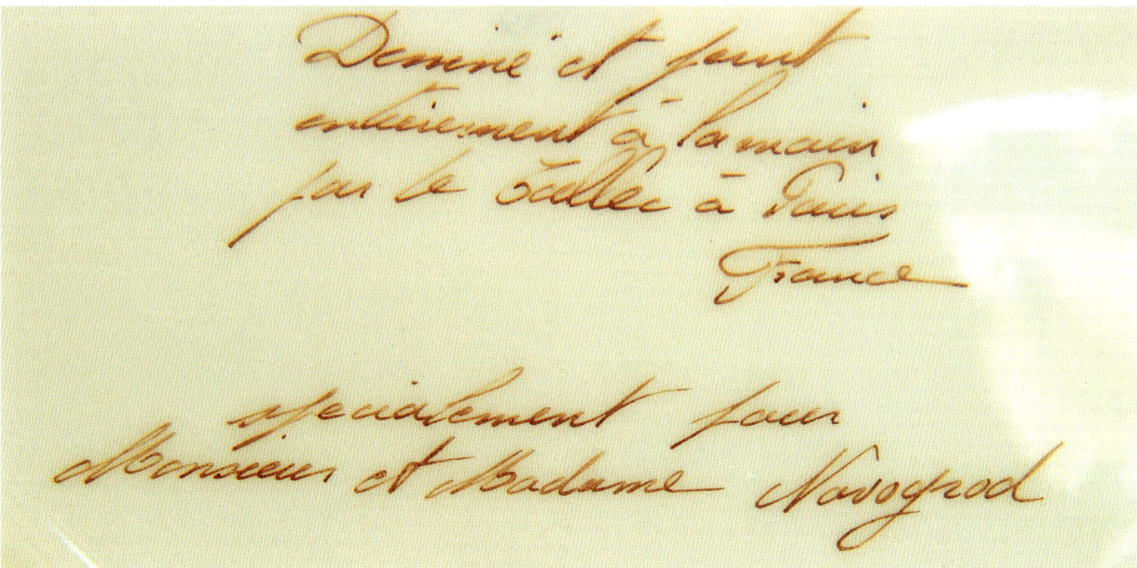

Plate and Mark, 10.1" in diameter, *Trois Médaillons de Sèvres*, a special order for the Sèvres museum and marked *Adaptation of a Soft-Paste Porcelain Plate Made at the Royal Manufactory at Sèvres, about 1770*. See photograph of mark.

Cup and Saucer, cup, 2.5" high x 3.75" in diameter and saucer, 5" in diameter, *Napoleon III*, AA/GD. Up to $500

Cup and Saucer, cup. 2.5" high and saucer, 5.25" in diameter, *Médaillons Fleurs sur Fond Bleu*, no marks. Up to $500

Cup and Saucer, cup. 2.5" high and saucer, 4.75" in diameter, *Médaillons Corail sur Fond Gris*, ZZ/MC. Up to $500

Cup, 2.25" high, *Fleurs sur Fond Noir Marbré*, YY/GD. Up to $500

Cachepot, 7" high x 9.5" handle to handle, *Cartel de Fleurs Fond Pourpré avec Rinceaux Or*, LL/JJ. $500-$1,000

Cup and Saucer, cup, 2.25" high and saucer, 4.75" in diameter, *Fleur de Lys*, MM/SF. Up to $500

Cup and Saucer, cup, 2.5" high and saucer, 4.5" in diameter, *Semis de Fleurs*, DD/RB. Up to $500

Cup and Saucer, cup, 2.25" high and saucer, 5.1" in diameter, RR/CH. $500-$1,000

Plate, 9.75" in diameter, *Semis Rouge*, BB/JL. Up to $500

Below:
Cup and Saucer, cup 2.25" high and saucer, 5.1" in diameter, *Fleurs Bande Bleue*, TT/LH. $500-$1,000

Cup and Saucer, cup 2.5" high and saucer, 5.25" in diameter, *Five Médaillons*, *v*/GM. $500-$1,000

Jardinière and Plates, jardinière, 9.5" high x 12" at widest point and plates, 9.5" in diameter, τ/GM, from a collection called, *Fleurs de Lune*, designed by E. Thuraner, a designer who was not part of the studio. See photograph of mark. $1,500-$2,000 for jardinière and $500-$1,000 each for plates

Plates, 8.5" in diameter, *Fleurs à la Manière de Meissen*, very popular theme in the 1970s, II/SHF and II/GD. Up to $500 each

Fleurs sur Fond Gris

The *Fleurs sur Fond Gris* pattern reflects the late eighteenth century love of nature. The flowers in this pattern are not presented in a rigid arrangement but are scattered to reflect a pleasant array of field flowers, which can be found in the countryside outside Paris. This type of pattern was originally created in 1790 by the Paris manufacturer, Guerhard & Dihl, at the end of the royal patronage of the Duc D'Angouleme. According to John Loring, the "floral patterns are Europeanized descendants of the traditional flower motifs of the lacquered papier-mâché imported from Kashmir" (*Tiffany Taste*).

Cup and Saucer, cup. 2.25" high x 3.5" in diameter and saucer, 5.75" in diameter, *Fleurs sur Fond Gris* (Tiffany pattern), RJ/SHF. Up to $500 each

Box, 2.5" high x 5.25" x 3.5", *Fleurs sur Fond Gris* (Tiffany pattern), S/FE. Up to $500

Fleurs sur Fond Noir

Fleurs sur Fond Noir was designed by Mr. Le Tallec and Tiffany & Co. design director, John Loring. The floral bouquets in this pattern were taken from several Napoleon III style porcelain pieces. The richly colored flowers contrast sharply with the deep black shoulder of the plate, which make this pattern more contemporary.

Cup and Saucer, cup, 2.1" high and saucer, 4.5" in diameter, *Fleurs sur Fond Noir* (Tiffany pattern), RV/SHF on cup and RX/SH on saucer. Up to $500

Guirlande de Fleurs

This unique pattern derives from the latter period of King Louis XV, c. 1770, at the time Madame du Barry was his mistress. The graceful sweep of spring garlands complements the scalloped edge of the plates, with the garlands falling between the "scallops" of the blank from the dark blue border around the edge.

Plate, 10.25" in diameter, *Guirlande de Fleurs* (Tiffany pattern), RS/SM. $500-$1,000

Box, 5.1" x 8.4", *Guirlande de Fleurs Or in Relief*, UU/CC. $500-$1,000

Egg Box, 4", *Croisillons et Fleurs*, SS/GH. Up to $500

Perfume Bottle, 7" high, *Sous Bois*, marked G/LB and *MADE IN FRANCE EXCLUSIVELY FOR PARIS DECORATORE*. Up to $500

Plate, 11" in diameter, GG/LB, *Dentelle Fleurie* (Tiffany pattern), patterned after an antique plate from Manufacture de Clignancourt, which was in Mr. Le Tallec's collection. $1,000-$1,500

Cup and Saucer, cup, 2.25" high x 4" in diameter and saucer, 6" in diameter, *Myosotis Bleu*, XX/SHF. Up to $500

Cup and Saucer, cup, 2.6" high x 4" in diameter and saucer, 6" in diameter, *Bleuets*, MM/SHF. The *Bleuets* pattern became a Tiffany & Co. pattern in 2002. Up to $500

Cup and Saucer, cup, 2.3" high x 2.9" in diameter and saucer, 4.6" in diameter, *Bleuets*, SS/SHF. Up to $500

Bouillon Cup and Saucer, cup, 4.6" in diameter and saucer, 6.5" in diameter. Pattern was hand painted for King Hassan II, ξ/CG on cup and WW/MC on saucer.

Bowl, 8.25" in diameter, *Pastilles*, 8.25" in diameter, φ/AM. Up to $500

Plate, 10.1" in diameter, *Chrysantèmes* (Tiffany pattern), RRA/SHF. $500-$1,000

William IV

William IV was created to commemorate Tiffany & Co.'s 150th anniversary. It is an adaptation of an English pattern that was fashionable when Tiffany & Co. was founded in 1837. The pale "Tiffany blue" background is a distinguishing characteristic, which gives the pattern a light airy feeling.

Plate, 10.75" in diameter, *William IV* (Tiffany pattern), R?/SHF. $500-$1,000

Cup and Saucer, cup, 2.25" high and saucer, 6.25" in diameter, *William IV* (Tiffany pattern), cup marked RS/SHF and saucer marked RR/SHF. Up to $500

Bleu Céleste

This pattern was influenced by the bleu céleste of Madame de Pompadour, which was created for her in 1754 by Louis the XV's Royal Porcelain company located in Vincennes just outside of Paris. The Tiffany pattern was created from a "wave" patterned jardinière, which was created by Taillandier and in the private collection of Mr. Le Tallec. The extremely fine detailing of this majestic pattern is a superb demonstration of the skill of the painters at Le Tallec.

Plate, 10.25" in diameter, *bleu céleste* (Tiffany pattern), RL/GM. $500-$1,000

Salad Plate, 8" at widest point, *Bande Corail sur Bleuets*, MM/GD. Up to $500

Plate, 10.5" in diameter, pattern called *1900*, RR/SHF. Pattern was created about twenty years ago by the Tiffany & Co. studio but was never produced.

Escalier de Cristal

The prototype for this pattern comes from a cup and saucer made in the 1830s by Escalier de Cristal of Desamous, located in the Palais Royal in Paris. The original pattern was a Charles X design of "Fleurs sous Arcade". In *Escalier de Cristal*, the rich blue on the shoulder of the plate opens up into arcades, which frame ten different varieties of garden flowers.

Plate, 10.75" in diameter, *Escalier de Cristal* (Tiffany pattern), R?/SHF. $500-$1,000

Coral with Médaillons Flower

This pattern, created by Tiffany & Co. design director, John Loring, was inspired by a pair of mid-eighteenth century faience salt cellars, which featured médaillons of polychrome fleurettes. While the original design featured a background of blue, this interpretation places the floral médaillons against a rich coral background, creating a striking and pleasing contrast.

Plate, 9.25" in diameter, *Valse de Médaillons de Corail* (Tiffany pattern), YY/GM. $500-$1,000

Plate, 9.5" in diameter, *Marseilles*, an interpretation of a nineteenth century earthenware pattern from the Marseilles Faïencerie, RJ/GM. Up to $500

Cup and Saucer, cup, 2.25" high and saucer, 4.6" in diameter, *Chantilly*, TT/RG. $500-$1,000

Tea Cup and Saucer, cup, 2.25" high and saucer, 6" in diameter, *Décor Vieux Paris* (Tiffany pattern), cup marked WW/SHF and saucer marked K?/GD. Up to $500

Cup and Saucer, cup, 2.5" high and saucer, 5.75" in diameter, *Mennecy* (Tiffany pattern), MM/GD. Up to $500

Box, 6" square x 3.4" high, *Marie Thérèse*, WW/SHF. $500-$1,000

Cup and Saucer, cup, 2.4" high x 2.5" in diameter and saucer, 5" in diameter, *Pensees Violettes*, EE/MC or ML. Up to $500

Box, 2" high x 4.75" in diameter, no pattern name (Tiffany pattern), ?/AM.AC. Up to $500

Ashtray in three-footed brass frame, 1.75" high x 6" in diameter, *Bouquet*, α/MJ. Up to $500

Teapot and Cup and Saucer, Teapot, 8.5" from handle to spout x 4.5" high; cup, 4.75" x 2.5"; and saucer, 7.75" in diameter, *Papillons Normands* (Tiffany pattern), teapot, ε/CH and cup and saucer, α/SHF. $1,000-$1,500

Inkpot, 2.75" high x 3.75", *Flowers in Pink*, GG/GC. Up to $500

Box, 4.25" x 4", no pattern name (Tiffany pattern), α/FE. Up to $500

Cup and Saucer, cup, 2.25" high and saucer, 4.75" in diameter, *Chardons*, K?/AM. Up to $500

Ronsard

Created in 2000, this pattern is a symphony of gold roses engraved with an agate stone. It is inspired by the French poet, Pierre de Ronsard, who wrote many poems about roses.

Vase, 10" high, *Ronsard*, DC/CS. $500-$1,000

Plate, 10" in diameter, *Ronsard on Tile Colored Background*, DD/SP. $500-$1,000

Lubéron

Lubéron is the countryside of Avignon, France, where multiple kinds of flowers are grown. The pattern, created in 1998, shows bright flowers on a black shoulder.

Plate, 7.75" in diameter, *Lubéron*, DD/YM. Up to $500

Plate, 8.75" in diameter, *Poires sur Or* (Tiffany pattern), a prototype, DC/SHF.

Plate, 8" in diameter, *Vegetable Garden* (Tiffany pattern). Up to $500

Plate, 10" in diameter, *Three Médaillons on Croisillons*, HH/SHF, designed from an antique pieces in Mr. Camille's collection. $500-$1,000

Directoire

Directoire, named after the period between the French Revolution and the Napoleonic Empire, reflects the era's taste for neoclassic design. While the inspiration for the design is quite formal, the warm earth tone colorings and flowing curves of the pattern make it easily adaptable for either formal or informal settings.

Plate, 8" in diameter, *Directoire* (Tiffany pattern), VV/CH. Up to $500

Fontainebleau Box, *Directoire* (Tiffany pattern), ?/MP. $500-$1,000

Plate, 10.1" in diameter, *Clairière*, GG/SHF. $500-$1,000

Lighter, 5" tall x 2.5" in diameter, *Croisillons Rose*, JJ/SF, and marked, *Bonwit Teller*. Up to $500

Ashtray, 5" x 3.75", *Croisillons*, α/SF. Up to $500

Box, *Croisilloné Bleu*, 3.5" x 2", VV/LC. Up to $500

Foliage Patterns

Valet Tray, 6" x 4.4", *Feuilles de Chêne*, YY/JLC. Up to $500

Cachepot, 4.5" high x 4.5" in diameter, *Feuilles de Chêne*, ξ (1971)/SHF. Up to $500

Bowl, 2.1" high x 7" x 8.25", Feuilles de Chêne, RH/SG and marked Hand painted in France by Le Tallec, Paris for Saks Fifth Avenue. $500-$1,000

Cup and Saucer, cup, 2.5" high and saucer, 4.5" in diameter, *Bay Leaves*, OO/CJ. $500-$1,000

Cup and Saucer, cup, 2.25" high and saucer, 4.75" in diameter, *Feuilles de Chataigniers sur Fond Gris*, II/GD. Up to $500

Cup and Saucer, cup, 2.4" and saucer, 4.75" in diameter, *Chardons*, K?/AM. $500-$1,000

Ginger Jar, 9.5" high, *Viaduc des Arts*, DB/CS, a limited edition pattern, which was sold only by the studio's onsite boutique shop to celebrate the opening of the studio to the public. $2,000-$2,500

Plate, 7.75" in diameter, a Musée des Arts Décoratifs pattern, RT/SHF. Up to $500

Plate, 8" in diameter, *Red Vine* (Tiffany pattern), RD/GM. Up to $500

Below:
Cup and Saucer, cup, 2.25" high and saucer, 4.75" in diameter, *Feuilles Rouges*, K?/AM. $500-$1,000

Cup and Saucer, cup, 2.1" high and saucer, 5" in diameter, *Palmettes* (Tiffany), OO/AM. $500-$1,000

Bonbon, jar, 8.5" high x 4.5" in diameter and plate, 8" in diameter, *Florentin*, OO/MC. $2,000-$2,500

Soup Tureen, bowl, 11" high x 14" handle to handle and plate, 14.5" handle to handle, *Marin on Yellow*, CC/MC. $5,000+

Plate, 10.25" in diameter, *Marin on Yellow*, α/CC. $500-$1,000

Plate, 6.25" in diameter, plain yellow to match *Marin on Yellow* pattern, DF/CS and marked *Thomas and Keith*. (Painter Claude Coudec [CC] married in 1969 and became painter Claude Souffron [CS].) Up to $500

Tray, 4.75" x 2.75", *Marin in Gold Relief on White*, β/AD. Up to $500

Orange Juice Pitcher and Tray, pitcher, 12.5" high and tray, 12.75" in diameter, *Marin in Gold Relief on White*, GG/DD. $2,000-$2,500

Close up of *Marin in Gold Relief on White* pattern.

Cup Directoire and Saucer, cup, 3.6" x 3" and saucer, 5.4" in diameter, *Marin on Cobalt*, ω/CS. $500-$1,000

Cup and Saucer, cup, 4.25" high x 3.5" in diameter and saucer, 5.5" in diameter, *Marin sur Pourpre*, W/CS. $500-$1,000

Bonbon, covered dish, 9" high and plate, 9" in diameter, *Acanthe*, DD/GD, and marked, *specialement pour La Marquise de Sévigné*, a famous candy store in Paris on avenue Victor Hugo, which closed five years ago. The technique used to decorate this piece is time-consuming. First the "white" areas are protected with a water-soluble resin, and then the color pigment is mixed with a raised paste, turpentine and oil and applied evenly over the surface. After it has dried, the resin, or "resist" is removed. Once the paste containing the color has been fired, any remaining decoration can be done. $2,500-$3,000

Jar, 18" high, *Bacchus*, DA/CS. $2,000-$2,500

Ice Bucket, 7.5" high, *Bacchus*, DC/YM. $1,500-$2,000

Box, 2" high x 5.25" x 3.5", *Treille Muscate*, υ/MFM. $500-$1,000

Bonbon Dish, 5.75" high, *Treille Muscate*, RRE/SM. $500-$1,000

Cachepot, 4.6" high x 6.5" handle to handle, *Treille Muscate*, dated YY. Up to $500

Plate, 10.1" in diameter, *Treille Muscate*, M/SFM. $500-$1,000

Clairette Box, 2.1" high x 2.1" in diameter, *Treille Muscate*, RZ/SHF. Up to $500

Box, 4.5" x 3", *Treille Muscate, Fleurs au Centre*. $500-$1,000

Clairette Box, 2.1" high x 2.1" in diameter, *Treille Muscate with Gold Relief*, RO/PP. Up to $500

Bonbon, bowl, 9.25" high and plate, 9" in diameter, *Treille Muscate with Gold Relief*, μ/FG. $1,000-$1,500

Clairette

Mr. Le Tallec created this pattern to commemorate the birth of his granddaughter, Claire, in 1982. The pattern is decorated in either pink or light blue flowers with gold foliage.

Coffret Box, 3" x 1.5", *Clairette*, α/SF. Up to $500

Cup and Saucer, from an original design for the Musée des Arts Décoratifs. See photograph of mark at right. Up to $500

Charger, 12" in diameter, *Vignes*, DA/SHF, special order for Marlo Thomas from Tiffany & Co. See photograph of mark.

Cup and Saucer, cup, 3.5" high and saucer, 5.6" in diameter, *Joyaux*. The mark indicates the pieces were possibly hand painted by Mr. Le Tallec's mother in 1928.

Cup and Saucer, cup, 2.25" high and saucer, 4.6" in diameter, no pattern name, φ/SF, marked *Bonwit Teller*. Up to $500

Cup and Saucer, cup, 2.5" high and saucer, 4.6" in diameter, GG/ML. Up to $500

Cup and Saucer, cup, 2.5" high and saucer, 5" in diameter, *Restauration*, GG/SHF. $500-$1,000

Plate, 8.6" in diameter, PP/SHF. Up to $500

Geometric and Abstract Patterns

Coeurs Fleuris

Inspired by Delftware, Coeurs Fleuris was originally created in the early nineteenth century by Mr. Blacheron of Porcelaine de Paris who combined several Dutch patterns. The pattern incorporates a strong geometric scallop design with the dominant "Tiffany yellow" to accent a graceful chain of gold hearts. The sprigs of flowers placed within each heart create a feel that is formal, yet fresh and youthful.

Plate, *Coeurs Fleuris* (Tiffany pattern). Up to $500

Coffee Pot, *Coeurs Fleuris* (Tiffany pattern). $1,000-$1,500

Pitcher, *Coeurs Fleuris* (Tiffany pattern). Up to $500

Box, *Coeurs Fleuris* (Tiffany pattern). Up to $500

Ashtray, 6.4" x 4.6", *Grignan Vert*, RRB/MYB. Up to $500

Bonbon, 7" high x 8.5" handle to handle, *Grignan Vert*, TT/SF. $1,000-$1,500

Plate, 10.25" in diameter, *Grignan Vert*, RR/MFM. $500-$1,000

Box, 4.5" x 1.9", *Grignan Bleu*, ζ/AL. Up to $500

Ashtray, 5" x 3.75", *Grignan Rouge*, π/AL. Up to $500

Plate, 10.25" in diameter, *Grignan Bleu*, LL/SF. $500-$1,000

Cup and Saucer, cup, 2.4" high x 2.3" in diameter and saucer, 4.75" in diameter, *Grignan Rose* (Tiffany pattern), HH/GD. $500-$1,000

Vase, 12.5" high, *Gold Stones on Cobalt*, no mark, pre-1940. $2,500-$3,000

Left:
Cup and Saucer, cup, 2.25" high and saucer, 4.75" in diameter, *Losanges en Or*, WW/SHF. $500-$1,000

Plate, 10.5" in diameter, *Symphonie de Losanges* (Tiffany pattern), XX/SHF. $500-$1,000

Egg Boxes, 3.75" high x 2.6" in diameter, *Bandes de Couleur*, DC/VD. Up to $500

Plate, 8.75" in diameter, *Rayonnant Rouge*, MM/SHF. Up to $500

Plate, 7.75" in diameter, *Écossais*, RI/SHF, special order. See painting on back rim of plate and mark. Up to $500

Cup and Saucer, cup, 2.25" high and saucer, 6" in diameter, *Framboise Rose* (Tiffany pattern), cup marked RI/ALT and saucer marked α/AC. According to the studio, this was not a very popular pattern. Up to $500

Left:
Cup and Saucer, cup, 2.25" high and saucer, 4.6" in diameter, *Écossais*, λ /SHF. $500-$1,000

Cup and Saucer, cup, 2.25" and saucer, 5.1" in diameter, *Ecailles Roses*, cup, SS/SHF and saucer, β/CH. Up to $500

Plate, 10.5" in diameter, *Ondine*, DE/SHF. Originally designed in 1996, this pattern was rejected by the studio, and no pieces were sold to the public.

Panache

Panache is a modern interpretation of a Sèvres pattern painted in 1767 by Boulanger le Père. In the late eighteenth century, the ostrich feather crest, also known as a "panache," was a symbol of nobility. The Le Tallec pattern retains a formal and noble tone in its use of cobalt and gold, but the sweep of the feather motif gives it a light and fanciful feel.

Cup and Saucer, cup, 2" x 2.5" and saucer, 4.75" in diameter, *Panache* (Tiffany pattern), V/MF. $500-$1,000

Cup and Saucer, cup, 2.25" high and saucer, 5.1" in diameter, *Panache*, first version, RV/SHF. $500-$1,000

Cup and Saucer, no pattern name, RL/GP. Up to $500

Plates, 9.4" in diameter, ω/FM, no pattern name, designed by E. Thuraner, an outside designer. See photograph of mark. $500-$1,000 each

Plumes

Plumes was adapted from an early nineteenth century English pattern. It was created by Tiffany & Co. design director, John Loring. The design is a light, stylized feather, which gives the pattern a less formal feel than those created in the nineteenth century; however, with the ordered spotting of gold and powdering of feathers, the pattern retains the traditional nineteenth century flavor.

Plate, 8" in diameter, *Plumes* (Tiffany pattern), AF/GM. Up to $500

Plate, 7.75" in diameter, RB/CS, a prototype for Tiffany.

Plate, 9.25" in diameter, YY/AM, a prototype for Tiffany.

Plate, 9.25" in diameter, *Grains de Riz*, WW/AM. Up to $500

Plate, 10.25" in diameter, Christmas plate, RB/ALT, a prototype. Up to $500

Plate, 10.25" in diameter, *Marbré* (Tiffany pattern), RD?/ALT. Up to $500

(2) Cup and Saucer, cup, 2.25" high x 2.25" in diameter and saucer, 4.6" in diameter, *Marbré* (Tiffany pattern), ZZ/GD. Up to $500

Plate, 6.5" in diameter, *Pointillisme*, RN/SG.
Up to $500

Charger, 12" in diameter,
Puzzle Yellow, DC/CV.
$500-$1,000

Animal, Sea Life, and Insect Patterns

Candlestick, 5" high, *European Cat*, RG/G. $500-$1,000

Plate, 10" in diameter, *Farmyard*, DF/MFM. Up to $500

Black Shoulder

While the black band or rim, "shoulder," of the plate gives the pattern a modern feel, the inspiration for the design came from the fanciful murals unearthed at the ruins of Pompeii. These murals, discovered in the late eighteenth century, include images of trees, birds, insects, and animals against black backgrounds. These Pompeian themes had a great influence on neoclassical French design, which is exemplified by the 1810 porcelain prototype for this pattern. The pattern was first painted in 1956 or 1957. Over time the studio modified some of the animals in the pattern.

Cup and Saucer, cup, 3.5" to top of handle and saucer, 5" in diameter, *Black Shoulder*, first version, EE/AM. $500-$1,000

Opposite page, top:
Rolling Egg Box, Large Egg Box, Cachepot, Clairette Box, Creamer. *Black Shoulder* (Tiffany pattern), rolling egg box, 2" x 1.5", unmarked; large egg box, 3", ξ/JN; cachepot, 3.5" x 2.75", RR/MM; clairette box, 2", α/MM; and creamer, 2" x 1.5", RR/MYB. $500-$1,000 for cachepot and up to $500 each for others.

Meat Platter, 22.75" x 9", *Black Shoulder* (Tiffany pattern), RRB/JD. $1,500-$2,000

Jardin

This pattern was first created by the studio in 1996. Originally the design only included herbs and butterflies in gold. When Tiffany & Co. decided to add it to their "Private Stock" collection, they asked the studio to include dragonflies, turtles, salamanders, and ladybugs to complement the company's new nature jewelry line.

Plate, *Jardin* (Tiffany pattern). Up to $500

Covered Pot, *Jardin* (Tiffany pattern). $500-$1,000

Cup and Saucer, *Jardin* (Tiffany pattern). Up to $500

Box, *Jardin* (Tiffany pattern). Up to $500

Box, *Jardin* (Tiffany pattern). Up to $500

(18) Plate, 6.5" in diameter, *Nil*, new pattern being developed for Tiffany & Co., RR/SHF.

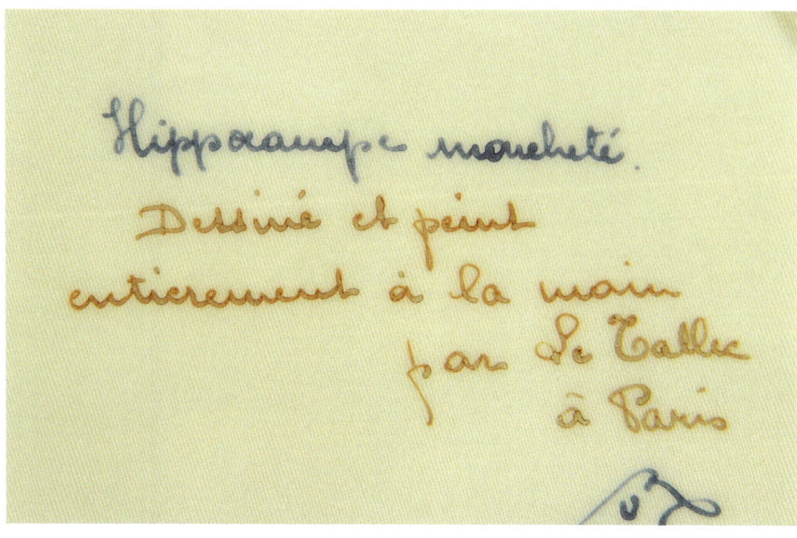

Plate, 10.5" in diameter, *Seahorse*, designed by Touchagues, a designer who was not part of the studio. The studio has no background information on this designer, V/GM. See photograph of mark. $500-$1,000

Plate, 10.5" in diameter, *Tiger Fish*, designed by Touchagues, V/GM. $500-$1,000

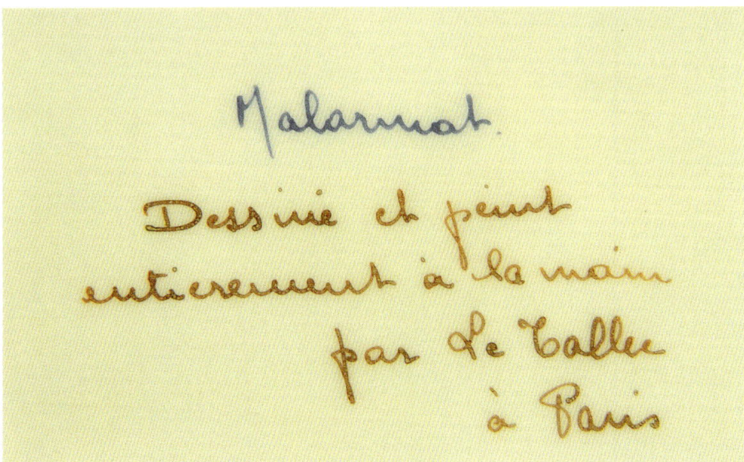

Plates, 9.5" in diameter, *British Fish* and *Seafood* respectively, 1967/GM, painted by Georges Marchand. See photograph of mark of *British Fish*. Up to $500 each

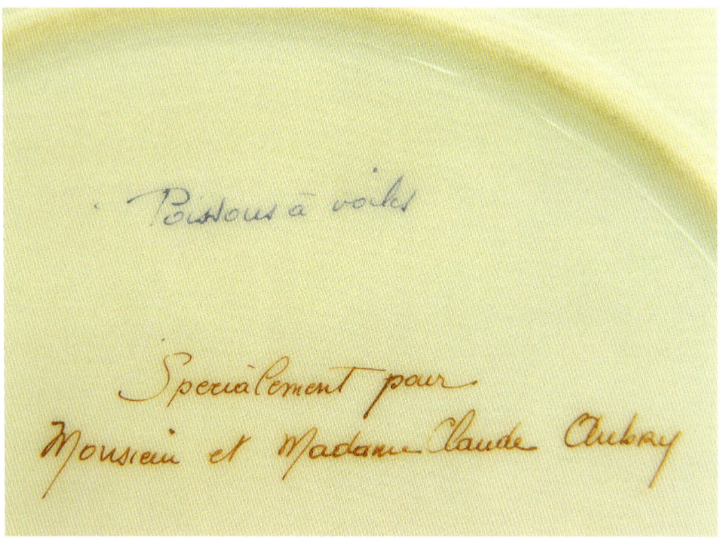

Plate, 10" in diameter, *Poisson en Or* (Tiffany pattern), PP/GD. Up to $500

Plate, 10" in diameter, (Tiffany pattern) a prototype, DC/CS. Up to $500

Tray, 3.25" x 3.25", *Insectes*, WW/LC. Up to $500

Box, 3.5" x 2.5", *Insectes* (Tiffany pattern), a variation, RE/PP. Up to $500

Abeilles Or

Bees are the symbol of Napoleon, and the original pattern was created by Sèvres in the early nineteenth century for the coronation of Napoleon.

Empire Vase, 3" high, *Abeilles Or*, ?/CL. Up to $500

Plate, 10.25" in diameter, *Papillons Normands*, RN/PP. Up to $500

Plate, 9.25" in diameter, *Papillons Normands* (Tiffany pattern), XX/PP. Up to $500

Cup and Saucer, cup, 2" high and saucer, 5.75" in diameter, *Papillons à La Française*, Q?/PP. Up to $500

Box, 3.5" x 2", *Papillons en Or*, DC/MYR. Up to $500

Other Patterns

Attributs de Musique

Based upon an eighteenth century pattern, this Le Tallec interpretation depicts musical instruments, such as guitars and violins. Pieces come in different colored backgrounds. There is also a garden story in this same basic pattern.

Apothecary Jar, 12.25" high, *Attributs de Musique*, W/GK. $2,000-$2,500

Elephant Box, 6.75" high x 5.1" square, *Attributs de Musique*, DA/VD. $1,000-$1,500

Box, 7.5" x 5" x 3" high, *Attributs de Musique*, ι (1971)/CS. $500-$1,000

(3) Mocha Coffee Cup and Saucer, cup, 1.5" high and saucer, 3.5" square, *Attributs de Musique*, DA/CV, made for cup collectors. Up to $500

Cup and Saucer, cup, 2.5" high and saucer, 5.1" in diameter, *Attributs de Musique*, ξ/MC. Up to $500

(26) Cup and Saucer, 2.5" high x 2.25" in diameter and saucer, 5" in diameter, *Mauresque*, "Sèvres" mark with *C* in middle, prior to 1940.

Below:
Trembleuse, cup, 6" high x 7.5" handle to handle and plate, 8.4" in diameter, *Grisé à la Manière de Boucher*, OO/HG. *Boucher* was a famous painter in the eighteenth century who also worked at Sèvres. This pattern was made at Sèvres during the reign of Louis XV, and it may have been made for Madame de Pompadour who liked angels. In the eighteenth century, the trembleuse was used by ladies to drink chocolate, which was taken as a prescription for various illnesses. The cup has a top to help avoid spilling the chocolate on the women's crinoline dresses. The pieces decorated at Le Tallec were sold as separate items and not part of a larger set; and the cups and saucers were purchased separately from different Limoges manufacturers. Following the tradition of the trembleuse as a container for chocolate, the Le Tallec trembleuses were often given as a "candy box" filled with chocolates. $500-$1,000

Trembleuse, cup, 4.25" high x 7.1" handle to handle x 5" in diameter and saucer, 8.1" in diameter, *Grisé à la Manière de Boucher*, cup, CC/AG and saucer, 8.1" in diameter. $500-$1,000

Crépuscule des Dieux

Named after a Wagner opera, this pattern depicts a drama, and its neoclassical design comes from Greek frescos. The figures are black and gold on a white background.

Plate, 10" in diameter, *Crépuscules des Dieux*, RR/CS. Up to $500

Charger, 12" in diameter, *Crépuscule des Dieux*, RR/CS. Up to $500

Cup and Saucer, cup, 2.25" high and saucer, 5.5" in diameter, *Incrustés d'Or*, LL/JL. $500-$1,000

Cachepot, 6" x 8", *Incrustés de Platine*, FF/DL. $1,000-$1,500

Plate, 10" in diameter, date mark unclear/ML, special order piece with name of customer.

Cup and saucer, cup. 2.5" high and saucer, 4.6" in diameter, *Bleuets and Vases Médaillons*, RR/SHF. Up to $500

Plate, 9.75" in diameter, *Bleuets and Vases Médaillons*, RR/SHF. Up to $500

Cup and Saucer, cup, 2.5" high and saucer, 5.1" in diameter, *Revolution*, RV/SHF. $500-$1,000

Plate, 10.1" in diameter, *Landscape* (Tiffany pattern), UU/GM, a very old and difficult technique is used to achieve the look of wood. $500-$1,000

Charger, 15.75" in diameter, *Palace of Versailles*, RR/G. $1,500-$2,000

Table Centerpiece, bowl, 18" high x 20" x 13", *Palace of Versailles*, BB/GM. $5,000+

Plate, 8.25" across, *Countryside*, no mark, painted by Georges Marchand. Up to $500

Plate, 15.9" in diameter, DC/YM, special order from a French customer and signed by an outside painter. See photograph of artist's signature.

Plate, 10.1" in diameter, *Scottish Landscape* (Tiffany pattern), a prototype, RRD/SHF. $500-$1,000

Berry Bowls, 5" in diameter, *Montgolfière*, FF/AG. Up to $500 each

Plate, 7.9" in diameter, *Cartes on Black*, RK/GM, a prototype.

Plate, 9" in diameter, *Cartes* (Tiffany pattern), RB/GM. Up to $500 each

Cup and Saucer, cup, 2.25" high x 2.25" in diameter and saucer, 4.75" in diameter, *Canasta* (Tiffany pattern), SS on cup and RR on saucer/GM. Up to $500

(22) Plate, 11" in diameter, *Canasta*, PP/GM. $500-$1,000

Cigar Box, 5" high, *Nicoletta Or*, VV/JN and marked *Bonwit Teller*. Up to $500

Apothecary Jar, 11.5" high, *Angoulême* [a city in France], PP/MC. $2,000-$2,500

Coffee Pot, 11" high, *Cobalt*, special limited edition order of fifteen pieces. See photograph of mark.

Plate, 10.5" in diameter, *Palmier Trois Médaillons*, RK/GM. Up to $500

Bowl, 8" in diameter, *Eyes of Partridge* (Tiffany pattern), UU/CH. Up to $500

Plate, 7.75" in diameter, *Duc de Mouchy* (Tiffany pattern), RD/FV. Up to $500

Above and left:
Consommé Cup and Saucer, cup, 7.75" handle to handle and saucer, 6.4" in diameter, special design for King Sidi Mohamed V, father of King Hassan II, K?/AM on cup and LL/MC on saucer. See photograph of mark.

Bigouden

Bigouden was derived from a highly popular early eighteenth century Delft pattern. The Delft original, located in the Musée des Arts Décoratifs in Paris, is painted in soft hues. Reinterpreting the design, Camille Le Tallec and former Tiffany design director, Mr. Van Day Truex, used an intense "French blue" and a more vibrant, bright yellow, "Tiffany yellow"—a color favored by Louis Comfort Tiffany.

Charger, 15.5" in diameter, *Bigouden*, ξ/SHF. $500-$1,000

Coffee Pot, Creamer and Sugar, pot, 8.5" high; creamer, 3.75" high at handle; and sugar, 1.9" high x 3.5" in diameter, *Dentelle Or*, Z/CLC. $1,500-$2,000

Box, 4.5" in diameter, *Arabesques in Gold Relief*, DD/SHF. $500-$1,000

Dessert Plate, 7.1" in diameter, marked *pour Marcel Rochas*, BB/SF. Rochas is a perfume company in France. According to the studio, this was an exclusive design for them, which they sold in their store in Paris. Only a few pieces of this pattern were painted. Up to $500

Cup and Saucer, cup, 2" high and saucer, 4.4" in diameter, *Plain Cobalt, Intérieur Or*, no date or painter marks, pre-1941. Up to $500

Plate, 10" in diameter, *Planètes*, MM/AM. Up to $500

Jar, *1900,* "Art Deco," size and marks not recorded. Up to $500

Plate, 10.25" in diameter, pattern not identified, RR/SHF, and marked *Tiffany & Co.* Up to $500

Soleil 2000

A pattern for the millennium, the *Soleil* design has the sun dancing with the moon on a bright yellow background with blue luster.

Decanter, 10.5" high, DF/CG, and plate, 10" in diameter, *Soleil 2000*, pattern designed for the millennium, DF/CG for both decanter and plate. $500-$1,000 for decanter and up to $500 for plate

Bell, 3.5" x 2.5", *Sun is Dating the Moon*, only marks are *Tiffany & Co.* Up to $500

Plate, 6.25" in diameter, *Horoscope*, WW/HM. Up to $500

Coffret Box, 5" x 3", *Horoscope*, old version, GG/AM. Up to $500

Plate, 10" in diameter, *Paris, Paris*, DE/YM, prototype for a new design.

Clowns

This pattern was first designed in 1998 for a child's mug. The pattern became so popular that the studio is now using it on dinnerware and giftware. The figures represent the most famous clowns in France.

Charger, 12" in diameter, *Clowns*, DC/YM, a sample for the studio. $500-$1,000

Lulu

The design is like a cartoon, and the studio first created it just for fun to decorate their Christmas tree. It then became a popular pattern in the U.S.

Cup and Saucer and Creamer, cup, 2" high x 3" in diameter; saucer, 5.2" in diameter; and creamer, 4" high, *Lulu*, DC/YM. $500-$1,000

Boxes, 3" long x 2" in diameter, *Lemons* (made for Tiffany & Co.), dated 1981, prototypes made for the Musée des Arts Décoratifs. Blanks are no longer available.

Alice

This pattern was created in 1999, and it is an interpretation of the complete Alice in Wonderland story.

Plate, 6.5" in diameter, *Alice in Wonderland*, DC/YM, created by the studio in 1999. Up to $500

Plate, 12" in diameter, *Alice in Wonderland*, DC/YM, one of a set of six plates each with a different design. $500-$1,000

Charger, 12" in diameter, platinum service plate made for Tiffany & Co., DF/CO or CG. Up to $500

Boxes, cat, 3.1" high; elephant, 3.5" high; and fox, 2" high x 2.25" in diameter, *Animaux en Or*, all marked DD and painter CM for elephant and fox and painter VD for cat. Up to $500 each

Box, *Oeil de Perdrix Rose* (Tiffany pattern), RY/CM. Up to $500

Valse Bleue

Valse Bleue was inspired by a diamond shaped pattern found on porcelain in the Musée des Arts Décoratifs in Paris. The motif originated in Asia and later appeared in eighteenth century Chinese and Middle Eastern designs. In this Le Tallec pattern, the basic diamond design has been arranged with a garden motif and open fretwork so that the pattern appears to "waltz" around the shoulder of the plate in a lyrical fashion; hence the name, *Valse Bleue*. This pattern is also painted in red and called, *Valse Rouge*.

Octagonal Box, 2.5" x 2.5", *Valse Bleue* (Tiffany pattern), ξ/AC; Clairette Box, 2.1" x 2.1", *Princess Astrid* (Tiffany pattern), RN/AC; Round Box, 2.1" x 2.1", *Flower Pink*, NN/RG; Rectangular Box, 2.25" x 1.5", *Grignan Coral*, ?/SF; Heart Box, 3.5", *Nicoletta Pourpre*, L/HCR; Square Box, 2" square, *Baron Jourdan Bleu*, RB/TP.

Remainder of Fifty-two Important Patterns with No Photographs

There were five of the fifty-two important patterns, as identified by the studio, that we were unable to photograph. Following is the background on these five patterns:

Charmille (Le Tallec). The inspiration for this pattern came from an old wallpaper design in a castle in Normandy. The gold ivy leaves are trailing on the plates like they trail on a wall. The pattern is especially nice on vases and cachepots.

Josephine (Le Tallec). This pattern incorporates bees and flowers on a green background. The original pattern was created by Sèvres for the Empress Josephine, wife of Napoleon, when she began decorating Malmaison, a small castle outside of Paris. She died there in 1814.

Palmier d'Or (Tiffany). *Palmier d'Or* was an adaptation by Tiffany & Co. design director, John Loring, from a selection of late eighteenth and early nineteenth century chinoiserie patterns. The palm tree motif, which was drawn from an Empire pattern created by Dagoty at Porcelaine de Paris, incorporates playing children into a traditional chinoiserie design.

Polka (Le Tallec). Created in 1995, this is one of the studio's first contemporary designs. The studio wanted a change from designing patterns based upon eighteenth and nineteenth century pieces, and they designed a pattern that would appeal to contemporary women who are engaged and who are selecting an initial dinnerware pattern.

Tulipes Royales (Tiffany). The pattern was created in 1998 and uses a luster pigment. It appears on large display vases at Tiffany & Co. flagship stores.

Auction of Camille Le Tallec's Personal Collection

The photographs in this section are taken from the 1990 auction catalogue of Mr. Le Tallec's private ceramic collection. (*See* Bibliography.) Many of these pieces served as inspiration for many Le Tallec patterns. The studio developed many patterns that were reinterpretations of these original patterns. Often, a Le Tallec pattern is based upon the designs of several different pieces. In looking over these pieces in Mr. Le Tallec private collection, it is often easy to identify the influences that resulted in many of the studio's patterns. When it is obvious, we have provided the name of the Le Tallec pattern that corresponds to the pattern of the original piece. We have also identified the manufacturer and the time period when these original pieces were made, as noted in the auction catalogue. The numbers in **bold** refer to the item numbers that identify numbered pieces within the photographs of the auction catalogue.

French Dating Periods

Charles X, 1622-1660
Revolutionary, 1789-1795
Directoire, 1795-1799
Romantic, end of eighteenth century to beginning of nineteenth century
Empire, 1804-1814

Cover of Ader Picard Tajan auction catalogue of Camille Le Tallec's collection. The house on the cover was Mr. Le Tallec's home, which was located between La Gare de Lyon and La Bastille in Paris in the 12th Arrondissement. The auctions in November 1990 totaled approximately $4 million, according to John Loring, design director at Tiffany & Co.

Display case in Mr. La Tallec's home.

All of these pieces are Vienne (hard paste porcelain) from the nineteenth century.

All of these pieces are Saxe (hard paste porcelain) from the eighteenth century.

Tournai (bone china), marked with swords in gold, eighteenth century.

No. 641, Tournai (bone china), eighteenth century.

No. 664, Bordeaux (hard paste porcelain), marked, eighteenth century.

Nos. 670-673, Strasbourg (hard paste porcelain), eighteenth century and **No. 674**, Strasbourg, Louis XVI period; decorator, Atelier de Joseph Hannong.

No. 682, Marseille (faïence), eighteenth century, Atelier de la Veuve Perrin—Le Tallec *Seafood* pattern.

No. 753, Strasbourg (faïence), eighteenth century, mark of Joseph Hannong—Le Tallec *Chinoiserie Pourpre* and other chinoiserie figural patterns.

Candlesticks, Mennecy (bone china), eighteenth century. These candlesticks are reminiscent of the candlestick blanks with Le Tallec chinoiserie patterns.

Nos. 792, 793, Sèvres (bone china), letter dated I, 1761, and **No. 783**, Vincennes (porcelaine tendre), letter dated D, 1756; decorator, Jean-Louis Morin I, 1754-87—Le Tallec partial médaillons, photo 14/24. **No. 795**, Sèvres (bone china), letter dated R, 1770—Le Tallec *Trois Médaillons de Sèvres* pattern.

No. 801, Sèvres (bone china) letter dated X, 1775; decorator Guillaume Noël—Le Tallec *Grignan* pattern. **No. 800**, Sèvres (bone china), letter dated P, 1768; decorator, Jean-Jacques Pierre II, 1763-1798—Le Tallec *Médaillons Corail sur Fond Gris* pattern.

No. 808, Sèvres (bone china), *oeil de perdrix* (eye of partridge), letter dated O, 1767; decorator, Boulanger Père—Le Tallec *Panache* pattern. **No. 809**, Sèvres (bone china), letter dated G, 1759; decorator, Joffroy (?), celestial blue—Le Tallec *Cartel de Fleurs Fond Pourpré avec Rinceaux Or* pattern and other Le Tallec patterns with floral bouquets. **No. 811**, Sèvres (bone china), *oeil de perdrix* (eye of partridge); decorator, Vincent, 1788-1800, rose background—Le Tallec *Bay Leaves* pattern.

Nos. 827-833 and **837**, Sèvres (hard paste porcelain), eighteenth century and **No. 871**, Sèvres (bone china), Revolutionary period.

No. 842, Sèvres (bone china), celestial blue, marked, eighteenth century—Le Tallec *Marie Thérèse* pattern.

No. 862, Sèvres (bone china) letter dated PP, 1793; designer, Guillaume Noël—Le Tallec *Écossais* pattern.

Sèvres (bone china) Revolutionary period—Le Tallec *Attributs de Musique* pattern.

No. 942 (all pieces), Porcelaine de Paris (hard paste porcelain), Empire period—Le Tallec *Ronde de Cygnes* pattern.

No.950, Porcelaine de Paris (hard paste porcelain), first third of nineteenth century—Le Tallec *Cartes* pattern.

Paris (hard paste porcelain), marked *Honoré à Paris*, first third of nineteenth century.

No. 961, Porcelaine de Paris (hard paste porcelain), Retour d'Egypte, Empire period—Le Tallec *Bacchus* pattern.

All of the pieces are Porcelaine de Paris (hard paste porcelain), and all are from the Romantic period, except No. 897, Charles X period and No. 998, Louis-Philippe period.

No. 1005, Bayeux (bone china), "fantastic Chinese birds, butterflies, and flowers of the Indies," Romantic period—Le Tallec *Bayeux* pattern.

No. 887, Porcelaine de Paris (hard paste porcelain), end of eighteenth century.

No. 885, Porcelaine de Paris (hard paste porcelain), Directoire period—Le Tallec *Florentin* pattern.

Nos.767 and **769**, Chantilly, (bone china), marked, eighteenth century—Le Tallec *Bleuets* pattern.

Sèvres, not marked, eighteenth century—Le Tallec *Nuits de Chine* pattern.

No. 852, Sèvres (bone china), letter dated S, 1771; decorator, Baudoin Père—Le Tallec *Madame du Barry, Ruban Rose* and other patterns.

Porcelaine de Paris (hard paste porcelain), Empire period—Le Tallec grape patterns.

Porcelaine de Paris, (hard paste porcelain), marked *Desarnaux à l'Escalier de Cristal à Paris*, Charles X period—Le Tallec *Escalier de Cristal* pattern.

Studio Photographs

The photographs in this section are a sampling of what the studio was like in the past and what it is like today.

Atelier Le Tallec display sign.

Painters' workshop at the studio's current location at Viaduc des Arts on 93-94 avenue Daumesnil.

Current staff at Atelier Le Tallec.

Tiffany & Co. catalogue of Le Tallec Private Stock.

Décors :

1 • Baron Jourdan
2 • Ondine
3 • Treille muscate fleurie
4 • Oiseaux polychromes sur or
5 • Bacchus
6 • Surf
7 • Abeille
8 • Laque de Chine
9 • Puzzle
10 • Bagatelle

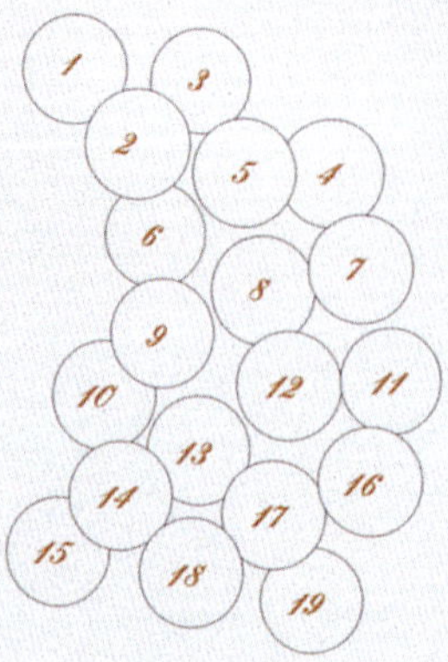

11 • Polka
12 • Tulipes sur or
13 • Grignan
14 • Ruban sur rose
15 • Duc de Mouchy
16 • Nicoletta
17 • Feux follets
18 • Marie Antoinette
19 • Josephine

Sales sheet of nineteen of Le Tallec's current patterns.

Palette Plate, 10.1" in diameter, RRC/CS, marked *Couleurs Johnson Matthey/Serie* 94, patterned after Jonson Matthey, England, one of the studio's pigment vendors.

Tiles painted by Georges Marchand for training of apprentices, each tile, 6" square, entire piece, 38.75" x 20.75", 1950. Mr. Marchand joined Atelier Le Tallec after WWII. Mr. Marchand left the studio about thirty years ago to join Sèvres. There has not been another male painter at the studio since Mr. Marchand left. According to studio lore, the women painters were quite fond of having a man as part of their group.

Le Tallec

REPRODUCTION DE
PORCELAINES & FAIENCES ANCIENNES
D'APRES DES PIECES DE MUSEE
ET DE COLLECTIONS PARTICULIERES

IVOIRES MINIATURES GRAVURES TEL. MENIL 67-63

9-11 RUE DES ENVIERGES ET 13-27 VILLA FAUCHEUR
PARIS XXE
R. C. SEINE 226 316
CH. POST PARIS 2174-17
PROD. SEINE N° 28.463

Conditions Générales de Vente. — Nos factures sont payables à Paris. En cas de contestation nous ne reconnaissons que la juridiction des Tribunaux de la Seine. Nos traites ou acceptation de règlement n'opèrent ni novation ni dérogation à cette clause attributive de juridiction. Il est spécifié que le non-paiement d'une seule traite à son échéance rend immédiatement exigibles, à notre gré, toutes sommes dues, sous quelque forme que ce soit pour la présente commande et toutes autres antérieures et nous donnent le droit d'annuler toutes commandes restant à livrer.

Atelier Le Tallec stationery from Villa Faucheur.

Staff at Atelier Le Tallec in 1950 at Villa Faucheur.

Painters' workshop at Atelier Le Tallec at Villa Faucheur.

Camille Le Tallec in the workshop showroom in 1978 at Villa Faucheur.

Arlette Le Tallec, Camille Le Tallec's second wife. This photograph was taken during a Catherinette party at the Le Tallec studio held on St. Catherine's Day. These parties are held for women employees who are not married by the age of twenty-five, Catherinettes. It is a tradition that the entire studio has to make a fancy hat, which the Catherinette wears at the party. Accompanied by prayer, the Catherinette will then find a husband before the following year's St. Catherine's Day. This tradition is especially strong in haute couture and in porcelain and crystal studios.

Camille Le Tallec in 1978.

Inside of church at St. Etienne in the Loire region. The paintings on lava on the wall of the church are the only pieces Camille Le Tallec ever painted himself, other than the watercolors which served as sources for the studio's patterns.

Stained Glass Window à la Manière de Le Tallec

These stained glass windows, which are in the authors' home, were created by Harmony Art Glass in Chicago based upon three different Le Tallec patterns. The cranes in the smaller panels are from the *Princess Astrid* pattern. In the wide panel, the bird on the left and the flowers are based upon the *Bayeux* pattern and the bird on the right is based upon the *Oiseaux de Sèvres* pattern.

Bibliography

There is very little published material on Atelier Le Tallec. It is our hope that this bibliography will grow considerably over the next few years.

Branch, Gigi. *Painting Birds on China.* Somerset, United Kingdom: Morton House, 1998.

_____. *Painting on China in the French Style.* Somerset, United Kingdom: Morton House, 1993.

Loring, John. *Tiffany's 150 Years*. Garden City, New York: Doubleday & Company, Inc., 1987.

Loring, John and Henry B. Platt. *The New Tiffany Table Settings*. Garden City, New York: Doubleday & Company, Inc., 1981.

Loring, John. *Tiffany Taste*. Garden City, New York: Doubleday & Company, Inc., 1986.

Tajan, Ader Picard. *Collections Le Tallec: Porcelaines et Faïences, Exceptionnelle collection de tasses principalement de Sèvres et Paris*. November 8 and 9, 1990. N.p.

"Tiffany: Invention et Qualité," *L'Oeil* (May 1968).

Index

This is an Index to the names of patterns (in italics) and individuals, manufactuers and stores, which are pertinent to the history of Atelier Le Tallec. Since the focus of this book is on patterns and their identification, we have not included in this Index the purpose of particular blanks, such as cups and saucers, bowls, etc. Also we have omitted page references to Tiffany & Co. since they are so numerous that it would be meaningless to list them.

Abeilles, 14, 59, 167
Acanthe, 131
Accrobate, 54
Afico, 45
Alice [in Wonderland], 6, 14, 199
Angoulême, 186
Animaux en Or, 200
Antoinette, Marie, 5, 86
Apothecary jars, *pots à pharmacie*, 10, 13, 14, 15-26, 38, 80, 93, 169, 412
Arabesques in Gold Relief, 191
Attributs de Musique, 14, 86, 169-171, 215
Aubepine Gold, 13
Automne Boisé, 14, 25, 69

Bacchus, 132, 217
Bagatelle, 14, 88-91
Ballet, 51
Bandes de Couleur, 146
Baron Jordan, 14, 85
Battle of Napoleon, 59
Bayeux, 14, 77-78, 219
Bayeux, Manufacture de, 77, 219
Bay Leaves, 124, 211
Bigouden, 7, 14, 190
Blacheron, Mr., 140
Black Shoulder, 8, 13, 14, 158-160
Bleu Céleste, 14, 111
Bleuets, 84, 108, 111, 177, 221
Bleuets and Vases Médaillons, 177
Bonwit Teller, 8, 122, 138, 185
Boucher, 172-173
Bouquet, 116
Bourgogne, 157
British Fish, 164
Buffon, 67

Canasta, 184-185
Carousel Chinois, 14, 37-38
Cartel de Fleurs Fond Pourpré avec Rinceaux Or, 98, 211
Cartes, 183-184, 216
Catherinette, 234
Castel Limoges, 8
Chantilly, 114
Chantilly, 221
Chardons, 117, 124
Charles X, 112, 203, 218, 225
Charmille, 14, 202
Chastagner, 8
Chinese Landscape, 31
Chinese Music Player, 46-47
Chinois, 26
Chinoiserie[s], 30, 31
Chrysantèmes, 109
Cirque Chinois, 7, 13, 14, 32-33
Clairette, 14, 136
Clairière, 122
Clignancourt, Manufacture de, 107
Clowns, 6, 14, 197
Cobalt, 187, 192
Coeurs Fleuris, 7, 14, 140-141
Couleurs Johnson Matthey/Serie, 94, 229
Comte d'Artois, 94
Corail Chinois [Coral de Chine], 14, 40
Coral with Médaillons Flower, 113
Countryside, 180
Crépuscule des Dieux, 14, 174
Croisilloné Bleu, 122
Croisillons, 106, 122

Danses Africaines, 48-49
Daumesnil, avenue, 6, 10, 226
Décor à la Rose, 84
Décor Vieux Paris, 114
de La Grange, Laurence, 4, 6, 39, 42
de Ronsard, Pierre, 118
Delft, 140, 190
Dentelle, 191
Dentelle Fleurie, 107
Directoire, 7, 14, 121
Duc D'Angouleme, 104
Duc de Mouchy, 189

Ecailles Roses, 148
Escalier de Cristal, 7, 14, 112, 225
Écossais, 147-148, 214
European Cat, 157
Éventails, 27
Eyes of Partridge, 188, 211

Faience, 80, 113
Famille Rose, 14, 45
Farmyard, 157
Feathers, 14
Feuilles de Chataigniers sur Fond Gris, 124
Feuilles de Chêne, 123
Feuilles Rouges, 126
Five Médaillons, 100
Fleurs à la Manière de Meissen, 102-103
Fleurs Bande Bleue, 100
Fleurs de Lune, 101
Fleur de Lys, 99
Fleurs 18 ème, 92, 93
Fleurs Japonaises, 44-45
Fleurs sur Fond Gris, 7, 14, 104
Fleurs sur Fond Noir, 14, 98, 105
Florentin, 127, 221
Flowers in Pink [Flower Pink], 117, 201
Fraise, Monsieur, 44
Framboise Rose, 148

GDA [Gérard, Dufraisseix, Abbot], 8
Gold Stones on Cobalt, 144
Grains de Riz, 154
Grignan, 141-144, 201, 211
Grisard, 58, 59
Grisé à la Manière de Boucher, 172-173
Guerhard & Dihl, 104
Guerre et Paix, 58-59
Guirlande de Fleurs, 14, 105-106

Halcyon, 7, 8, 14, 40
Harvest, 14, 82
Hassan, King, 7, 108, 189
Horoscope, 195
Hoving, Mr., 8

Imari, 40, 43-44
Incrustés, 175
Insectes, 166

Japon, 45
Jardin, 6, 13, 14, 160-161
Jardin de Chine, 14, 29
Jongleur, 54
Josephine, 14, 202
Joyaux, 138

Kimono, 41
Koi, 26

Ladies, 52-53
La Marquise de Sévigné, 64, 131
Landscape, 178
Laque de Chine, 27-28
Lemons, 198
Leopold II, King of Belgian, 70
Le Père, Boulanger, 150, 211
Le Tallec, Arlette, 234
Le Tallec, Camille, 4, 5, 7, 8, 9, 10, 13, 14, 15, 17, 32, 36, 40, 48, 51, 68, 70, 84, 92, 105, 107, 111, 136, 138, 190, 203, 234, 235
Loring, John, 4, 7, 8, 10, 40, 68, 104, 105, 113, 152, 202, 203, 238
Losanges en Or, 144
Louis XV, 82, 105, 172
Louis XVI, 38, 40, 54, 86, 208
Louvre, Musée du, 8, 94
Lubéron, 14, 119
Lulu, 6, 14, 198

Madame de Pompadour, 111, 172
Madame du Barry, 14, 82, 223
Madame du Barry, 82, 105
Marbré, 155
Marcel Rochas, 192
Marchand, Georges, 10, 61-63, 68, 164, 180, 230-231
Marin, 8, 127-130
Marin (boutique), 48
Marie Antoinette, 9, 14, 25, 86-87
Marie Thérèse, 115, 213
Marseilles, 113
Matthey, Johnson, 229
Mauresque, 172
Maximilien-Joseph, King of Bavaria, 188
Médaillons Corail sur Fond Gris, 97, 211
Médaillons de Fleurs, 80-81
Métiers de Paris, 54-56
Médaillons Fleurs sur Fond Bleu, 97
Mennecy, 114
Mennecy, 210
Modern Birds, 75
Montgolfière, 183
Morlent, Michel and Ginamy, 77
Musée des Arts Décoratifs, 31, 94, 125, 136, 190, 198, 201
Myosotis Bleu, 108

Napoleon III, 97
Nicoletta, 185, 201
Nil, 161
1900, 112, 193
Nuits de Chine, 14, 32, 38, 40, 222

Oiseaux Européens, 67-68
Oiseaux de Paradis, 66
Oiseaux Polychromes, 64-65
Oiseaux de Sèvres, 14, 64-66
Ondine, 149

Pagode, 41
Palace of Versailles, 179-180
Palmettes, 126
Palmier d'Or, 14, 202
Palmier Trois Médaillons, 188
Panache, 14, 150, 211
Paon, 76
Papillons à La Française, 168
Papillons en Or, 168
Papillons Normands, 116, 167-168
Paradise Birds, 74
Parisian View in 1850, 57
Paris, Paris, 196
Parrot, 60-63
Pastilles, 109
Pastorale, 14, 78
Peacock, 76
Pensees Violettes, 115
Perroquets, 75
Pillement, Jean, 6, 27, 41
Plain Cobalt, 192
Planètes, 193
Plumes, 152
Pointillisme, 156
Poires sur Or, 119
Poisson de Chine, 28
Poisson en Or, 165
Polka, 14, 202
Pompeii, 158
Porcelaine de Paris, 79, 92, 140, 202, 215, 216, 217, 218, 220, 221, 224, 225
Prince of Qatar, 7
Princess Astrid, 8, 14, 70-73, 201
Prototype Patterns, 75, 79, 119, 153, 154, 166, 182, 183, 196, 198
Puiforcat, 45
Puzzle Yellow, 156

Rayonnant Rouge, 146
Red Vine, 126
Restauration, 139
Revolution, 178
Ronde de Cygnes, 14, 79, 215
Ronsard, 14, 118
Roseraie, 84
Royal Limoges, 8
Ruban Rose, 83-84, 223
Rue de La Paix, 6, 9, 14, 39
Rue de Reuilly, 6, 7, 10, 15

Saks Fifth Avenue, 123
Scottish Landscape, 182
Seafood, 164, 209
Seahorse, 162
Semis de Fleurs, 99
Semis Rouge, 100
Sèvres, 7, 10, 17, 18, 38, 40, 64, 82, 85, 86, 88, 96, 150, 167, 172, 202, 210, 211, 212, 213, 214, 218, 222, 223, 230
Siam, 6, 14, 41
Sidi Mohamed V, King, 189
Soleil [2002], 14, 194
Souffron, Claude, 4, 128
Sous Bois, 106
Spanish Dancers, 49
Sun is Dating the Moon, 195
Symphonie de Losanges, 145

Taj Mahal [Râjastman], 6, 14, 42
Target, Jean, 51
Thomas, Marlo, 7, 137
Thuraner, E., 101, 151
Tiger Fish, 163
Toth, Jean, 48, 49
Touchagues, 52-53, 162, 163
Treille Muscate, 133-135
Trois Médaillons de Sèvres, 96, 210
Tulipes on Gold, 14, 92
Tulipes Royales, 14, 202

Valse Bleue, 14, 201
Van Day Truex, Mr., 190
Vegetable Garden, 120
Viaduc des Arts, 125
Vignes, 137
Villa Faucheur, 7, 10, 15, 232, 233, 234

Waterbrook-Clyde, Keith and Thomas, 78
William IV, 14, 110

Painters' Initials

Following is a list of the painters' initials found on the pieces in this book. Some of the letters of some of the initials were nearly illegible, so we took educated guesses when possible. Upon further study, it may be that we misread some of the letters in the initials. Most of those listed, however, are correct.

AC	FG	MFM
AD	FM	MJ
AG	FN	ML
AK	FV	MM
AKG	G	MMF
AL	GC	MP
ALT	GD	MYB
AM	GH	MYR
CB	GK	NB
CC	GL	OO
CCT	GM	PP
CG	GP	RB
CGM	HCR	RG
CH	HM	SD
CJ	JD	SF
CL	JJ	SFM
CLC	JL	SG
CLS	JLC	SH
CM	JN	SHF
CS	LB	SM
CV	LC	SP
DD	LH	TP
DL	MC	VD
FE	MCD	VM
FF	MF	YM

US $59.95
9 780764 317088 55995
ISBN: 0-7643-1708-3